THE UPPER ROOM.

WHERE THE WORLD MEETS TO PRAY

Susan Hibbins
UK Editor

INTERDENOMINATIONAL

INTERNATIONAL

INTERRACIAL

33 LANGUAGES

Multiple formats are available in some languages

CN00606386

The Bible Reading Fellowship
15 The Chambers, Vineyard
Abingdon OX14 3FE
brf.org.uk

The Bible Reading Fellowship (BRF) is a Registered Charity (233280)

ISBN 978 0 85746 605 1

Originally published in the USA by The Upper Room®
US edition © The Upper Room®
This edition © The Bible Reading Fellowship 2017
Cover image © Fraser Hall/Getty Images; map on page 6 © Thinkstock

Acknowledgements
The New Revised Standard Version of the Bible, Anglicised Edition, copyright © 1989, 1995 by the Division of Christian Education of the National Council of the Churches of Christ in the USA. Used by permission. All rights reserved.

Scripture quotations taken from The Holy Bible, New International Version (Anglicised edition) copyright © 1979, 1984, 2011 by Biblica. Used by permission of Hodder & Stoughton Publishers, an Hachette UK company. All rights reserved. 'NIV' is a registered trademark of Biblica. UK trademark number 1448790.

Extracts from the Authorised Version of the Bible (The King James Bible), the rights in which are vested in the Crown, are reproduced by permission of the Crown's Patentee, Cambridge University Press.

Extracts from CEB copyright © 2011 by Common English Bible.

Scripture quotations marked (TLB) are taken from The Living Bible copyright © 1971. Used by permission of Tyndale House Publishers, Inc., Carol Stream, Illinois 60188. All rights reserved.

Printed by Gutenberg Press, Tarxien, Malta

How to use *The Upper Room*

The Upper Room is ideal in helping us spend a quiet time with God each day. Each daily entry is based on a passage of scripture, and is followed by a meditation and prayer. Each person who contributes a meditation to the magazine seeks to relate their experience of God in a way that will help those who use *The Upper Room* every day.

Here are some guidelines to help you make best use of *The Upper Room*:

1   Read the passage of Scripture. It is a good idea to read it more than once, in order to have a fuller understanding of what it is about and what you can learn from it.
2   Read the meditation. How does it relate to your own experience? Can you identify with what the writer has outlined from their own experience or understanding?
3   Pray the written prayer. Think about how you can use it to relate to people you know, or situations that need your prayers today.
4   Think about the contributor who has written the meditation. Some *Upper Room* users include this person in their prayers for the day.
5   Meditate on the 'Thought for the day' and the 'Prayer focus', perhaps using them again as the focus for prayer or direction for action.

Why is it important to have a daily quiet time? Many people will agree that it is the best way of keeping in touch every day with the God who sustains us, and who sends us out to do his will and show his love to the people we encounter each day. Meeting with God in this way reassures us of his presence with us, helps us to discern his will for us and makes us part of his worldwide family of Christian people through our prayers.

I hope that you will be encouraged as you use the magazine regularly as part of your daily devotions, and that God will richly bless you as you read his word and seek to learn more about him.

Susan Hibbins
UK Editor

In times of/For help with...

Below is a list of entries in this copy of *The Upper Room* relating to situations or emotions with which we may need help:

Assurance: Jan 5, 16; Feb 6, 15, 24; Mar 6, 9, 28; Apr 20, 26, 28

Bible reading/study: Jan 4, 18, 26; Feb 6, 25; Mar 7, 11, 28; Apr 6, 7, 29

Change: Jan 1, 19; Feb 17, 20; Mar 25, 26; Apr 2, 6, 18, 19

Christian community: Jan 3, 9, 30, 31; Feb 5, 11, 28; Mar 28; Apr 11, 25

Christian example: Jan 11; Feb 3, 9, 10, 22; Apr 22

Compassion: Jan 23; Feb 1; Mar 12; Apr 18

Encouragement: Jan 12, 17, 24; Feb 4, 7, 22; Mar 10, 11

Evangelism: Jan 6, 14, 20, 25, 31; Feb 2, 10, 18; Mar 5, 27, 30; Apr 1, 25, 28

Family relationships: Jan 2, 5, 27; Feb 1, 3, 11, 27; Mar 3, 18; Apr 3, 5, 27

Fear: Jan 3, 12, 29; Feb 6, 13, 17; Mar 6, 18; Apr 18, 20, 23

Forgiving others: Mar 19, 26, 30; Apr 29

Giving: Jan 11, 17, 24; Feb 1, 22, 26; Mar 13, 23, 29

God's call: Jan 19, 21; Feb 2, 4, 28; Mar 1, 5, 22; Apr 18, 27

God's comfort: Mar 1, 17, 20

God's goodness/love/forgiveness: Jan 1, 6, 31; Feb 1, 3, 28; Mar 6, 8, 30; Apr 15, 18, 29

God's guidance: Jan 3, 7, 31; Feb 8, 9, 20; Mar 1, 8, 16, 20; Apr 8, 16, 26

God's presence: Jan 14, 18, 24; Feb 1, 6, 24; Mar 9, 16, 23; Apr 11, 21, 29

God's provision/strength: Jan 7, 15, 29; Feb 3, 26, 27; Mar 11, 17, 29; Apr 2, 3, 26

Gratitude/praise: Jan 1, 7, 17; Feb 2, 20, 27; Mar 4, 9, 29; Apr 11, 21

Grief/sorrow/loss: Mar 11, 21; Apr 2, 3, 5, 15, 18

Healing/illness: Jan 24; Feb 26; Mar 14, 31; Apr 3, 4, 15, 16

Insecurity: Jan 9; Feb 14; Mar 21

Jesus' example: Mar 30; Apr 27, 29

Joy: Jan 10, 23, 25; Feb 7, 25; Mar 6, 7, 23; Apr 11, 25, 29

Judging others: Mar 3, 13, 19

Lent: Mar 4, 11, 14, 18

Materialism/earthly distractions: Jan 16, 31; Feb 8, 19; Mar 4, 6

Mission/outreach/serving: Jan 6, 10, 25; Feb 1, 2, 16; Mar 1, 5, 23; Apr 3, 7

Obeying/listening to God: Jan 7; Feb 14, 21; Mar 1; Apr 3, 29

Peace: Jan 16, 18, 19, 22, 24; Feb 7, 8; Mar 11, 26, 27; Apr 9, 13, 14

Perseverance: Jan 9, 27; Mar 6, 9; Apr 4, 23

Prayer: Jan 3, 12, 22, 29; Feb 21; Mar 4, 7, 24; Apr 4, 6, 9, 30

Reconciliation: Mar 26; Apr 1, 2

Relationship with God/Christ: Mar 8, 26; Apr 16, 20, 27

Salvation: Jan 2, 26; Feb 5, 8, 25; Mar 6, 18, 31; Apr 1, 27, 28

Spiritual gifts: Jan 22; Feb 15

Spiritual growth through hard times: Jan 1, 21; Feb 6, 14, 20; Mar 11, 15; Apr 27

Spiritual restoration: Mar 4, 29; Apr 3, 19

Struggling with sin: Mar 19, 25; Apr 1

Transformation/new beginnings: Jan 1, 8; Feb 15; Mar 1, 4, 27, 30; Apr 2, 6, 27

Trusting God: Jan 3, 7, 9, 24; Feb 9, 12, 20; Mar 1, 15, 22; Apr 3, 12, 26

Working life/profession: Jan 7, 16, 21; Feb 3, 12, 27; Mar 5, 19, 22, 28

Worry: Jan 12, 16, 26, 29; Feb 20, 27; Mar 14, 15, 27; Apr 12

'Just as a body, though one, has many parts, but all its many parts form one body, so it is with Christ.'
1 Corinthians 12:12 (NIV)

Across from my desk is a bookcase with archive boxes lining the shelves, each with a label like 'Hindi', 'Italian', 'Japanese' and 'Portuguese'. It does not sound like an extraordinary sight; but when I look at it, I see the world. This bookcase is where I keep copies of international language editions of *The Upper Room* daily devotional guide. Publishing teams in Africa, Asia and Europe send me copies of every issue printed. Some copies arrive wrapped in newspaper and cloth that is sewn up to form a postal envelope, its corners sealed with red wax.

As I receive these copies, I often think about the many people who do the work of this ministry, the many hands that touch this 'little book'. I think of people all over the world sharing their faith stories in writing and submitting them for publication. I think of the editorial staff in Nashville, Tennessee, compiling the English manuscript for each issue of *The Upper Room*. I think of the publishing teams across the globe, many of them made up of volunteers, translating and editing the international editions. I think of the designers and printers producing copies of these editions and of the distributors posting and delivering them, some by motorbike and even on foot, to churches, hospitals, prisons, schools and homes of subscribers in more than 100 countries. I think of the millions of readers spending time with God in prayer through the pages of *The Upper Room* daily devotional guide.

Truly, we *are* many parts but one body! Together, we offer prayers in many languages; we serve God with a diversity of talents; and we worship in myriad different ways. My hope is that as you read *The Upper Room* you are blessed and transformed by our 'many-ness' and our oneness as people of faith!

Tia Runion
Manager, International Ministries, The Upper Room

ESTONIA
The Baltic Methodist Theological Seminary hosted an Upper Room writing workshop for students as part of an elective course called 'Communication of the Christian message to the general public'.

LEBANON
The Union of the Armenian Evangelical Churches in the Near East increased the number of donated copies of *The Upper Room* Armenian edition for Syrian-Armenian refugees with the help of donations from churches and individuals.

ESTONIA

LEBANON

Map © Thinkstock

The Editor writes...

I was with my husband having coffee in a crowded cafe, watching a very small boy play a game with his father. The child ran from where his father knelt with him to a counter-front on which were painted large flowers. He patted a flower with his little hand, chortled with glee, and then set off to run unsteadily back to his father, who opened his arms to envelop his son in a great hug, both of them laughing together. Then the child broke free to run back to his flower, repeating the process all over again. It was a lovely picture of a parent delighting in his child.

I thought about our relationship with our heavenly Father. So many times we go to him with our concerns for others and for ourselves, so many times we run to God when we are unhappy or in distress. It is right that we should, for Jesus invites us to do so: 'Come to me, all you who are weary and burdened, and I will give you rest' (Matthew 11:28, NIV). The Psalms, too, are full of prayers for help from people in the depths of despair.

How many times, though, I wondered, do we go to God when we are happy, when something wonderful has happened, and share that with him too? After all, God is concerned for every aspect and detail of our lives, not just the sad times: 'Even the very hairs of your head are all numbered' (Matthew 10:30, NIV). I believe that God is glad when, for example, our work goes well, when we complete a long-term project successfully or enjoy a happy family occasion.

The prophet Zephaniah sums this up:

'The Lord your God is with you, the Mighty Warrior who saves.

He will take great delight in you; in his love he will no longer rebuke you,

but will rejoice over you with singing' (Zephaniah 3:17, NIV).

What does it mean to you that God will 'rejoice over you with singing'? I think back to the child with his father in the cafe, and rejoice that our relationship with God can be just the same.

Susan Hibbins
UK Editor

The Bible readings are selected with great care, and we urge you to include the suggested reading in your devotional time.

Another year begins

Read Psalm 139:7–18

I praise you, for I am fearfully and wonderfully made. Wonderful are your works.
Psalm 139:14 (NRSV)

It's that time again, and I am ready to begin another new year. I have the same hopes for this year as I did for the last one: exercise more, get more sleep, eat healthier food, work more when needed and work less when I can.

Yes, this year will be the year that I make all these changes to improve my life!

But instead of jumping ahead too quickly, I decided to take some time to look back on this past year and celebrate my accomplishments. I suffered some real hardships and disappointments, but I made it through another year and grew from my adversities. Of course, I can always improve, and each year I make resolutions to be better. But I also know that I am a beloved child of God, who loves unconditionally. Nothing I can do will make God love me more or less.

So, as I look forward to the beginning of a new year, I am filled with new hope, expectations – and resolutions. And, as I look back on the past year, I celebrate my life and all that I have experienced, knowing that God has been with me through it all.

Prayer: *Dear God, help us to remember that we are your beloved children and that we can spread that love to all your children. Amen*

Thought for the day: God's love frees me to celebrate life with gratitude.

Andrea Woronick (Connecticut, US)

Jesus wept

Read John 11:32–35

When Jesus saw [Mary] weeping, and the Jews who had come along with her also weeping, he was deeply moved in spirit and troubled. 'Where have you laid him?' 'Come and see, Lord,' they replied. Jesus wept.

John 11:33–35 (NIV)

The phone call came in the middle of an ordinary morning. The caller was almost incoherent, overcome with grief. 'Ricky is dead.'

Ricky was my nephew. It was a freak accident, and now a man who was loved and who loved so freely was gone. He left behind a wife, stepsons, grandchildren, a mother, brothers and sisters, aunts and uncles, and friends. I struggled to make sense of it; I wanted to find a word of comfort for his mother. I wanted words of consolation for myself and for others who were hurting.

I found the words I needed in the passage about Lazarus in John 11: 'Jesus wept' – just two words but they were enough to remind me that God grieves with us. I didn't need the why of Ricky's death; I didn't need answers. What I needed was to weep with those who were weeping. The minister's words during the service celebrating Ricky's life were powerful. He reminded us that, as in the story of Lazarus, Christ brings us hope when we see no hope. Even in a time of grief, the promise of eternal life gives us strength to rejoice.

Prayer: *O God, help us to comfort those who hurt, to weep with those who weep and to rejoice with those who rejoice. In Jesus' name. Amen*

Thought for the day: In every moment, God can bring us hope and peace.

Jean Bonin (Alberta, Canada)

1,630 kilometres of prayer

Read 2 Corinthians 7:2–7

The Lord says, 'Do not fear, for I am with you, do not be afraid, for I am your God.'
Isaiah 41:10 (NRSV)

As I travelled with a group from my home country, Ukraine, to Russia for a festival celebrating the 125th anniversary of the Methodist Church in Eurasia, it was a time of great turmoil. Ukraine was experiencing a political, economic, and financial crisis – and even war. But as my group travelled the 1,630 kilometres to the festival, we truly felt the prayers of both our Ukrainian brothers and sisters at home and our Russian brothers and sisters who were waiting for us.

At each checkpoint, we were fearful that the guards would force us to turn around and go home since we were travelling with young men who were old enough to serve in the armed forces. But each time we were allowed to continue. At the last checkpoint before entering Russia, the border guards did not even look at our papers, which had caused many questions at other checkpoints. The guards just silently stamped our passports and let us through!

During our journey to the festival, I saw the hand of God leading us. We were fearful, but the difficulties we faced were no match for the power of God. Our trust in his faithful assistance helped us to overcome and to stand victorious.

How happy we were to arrive at the festival and to feel the loving arms of our brothers and sisters in Russia! We were a part of God's family of believers, whom no borders and no political, economic or financial problems could divide.

Prayer: *O God, thank you for journeying with us as we travel unknown paths. Help us to trust in you always. Amen*

Thought for the day: The more I trust God, the less I need fear.

Vasiliy Vuksta (Zakarpattia, Ukraine)

Resisting temptation

Read James 4:2–10

No temptation has seized you that isn't common for people. But God is faithful. He won't allow you to be tempted beyond your abilities. Instead, with the temptation, God will also supply a way out so that you will be able to endure it.
1 Corinthians 10:13 (CEB)

I was overjoyed. It was Friday and payday. But I had a problem. I had no money to get the bus to my job to pick up my money.

I thought long and hard and decided that I would try to pass off an old ticket, hoping the bus driver wouldn't notice. I walked to the bus stop, feeling sick about my decision. Facing this temptation to use deception, I thought of Joseph.

When Potiphar's wife tempted Joseph (Genesis 39:6–12), he didn't give in to the temptation. Instead, he ran from it. Joseph's response gives us all a model for when temptation is present. God will deliver a way out of temptation; we just have to take it. I prayed for God to help me, and just as he rewarded Joseph for resisting temptation, he rewarded me as well.

When the bus came, I walked on behind everyone else with my used ticket – and then I walked back off, deciding not to lie. The bus driver called after me and allowed me to travel that day for free. Sometimes our problems may seem unbearable and insurmountable without deceit, but God knows. If we prayerfully look for another way out of the situation, we can find it.

Prayer: *Dear Lord, teach us to trust you to give us strength when we face temptation. Amen*

Thought for the day: God provides a way when we resist temptation.

Ginger Robinson (Texas, US)

Never alone

Read Psalm 23:1–6

Jesus said, 'I am with you always.'
Matthew 28:20 (NIV)

I once took a train from the airport in Philadelphia to my sister's town 35 miles north. Though it was late at night, the train was crowded with people and more got on as we approached the city centre. As we proceeded north, more people exited than boarded and more and more seats became available. My destination was the last stop before the end of the line, and by the time we got there I was the only passenger left.

I liken this train ride to life's journey. During our childhood, we are surrounded by our family and friends. As the years pass, our family grows and our number of friends increases. But sooner or later, we begin to experience loss. One by one, family and friends pass away. As we travel through our senior years, more and more people dear to us exit our lives. If we live long enough, we may find ourselves the only remaining family member and with few, if any, close friends. But we have someone who will never leave us during life's journey: Jesus Christ. He has promised that he will always be by our side (see Matthew 28:20). He goes with us all the way to the end of the line, until we reach our heavenly home.

Prayer: *Good Shepherd, comfort us with the assurance that you will be by our side in each season of our lives. Amen*

Thought for the day: Jesus is with us at every stop on life's journey.

Wayne Greenawalt (Illinois, US)

PRAYER FOCUS: THOSE WHO ARE ELDERLY

What's new?

Read Revelation 21:1–5
The steadfast love of the Lord never ceases, his mercies never come to an end; they are new every morning.
Lamentations 3:22–23 (NRSV)

When my friends used to ask, 'What's new in your life?' I didn't know how to answer. I would think, 'What is happening in my life that is brand new? What can I tell them?'

But one day God gave me a new idea of how to respond. Now, when people ask me what's new in my life, I say: 'You know, absolutely everything is new.' I say that because today is a new day that will never happen again. And on this day, everything is new. Today there will be new insights from God, new encounters, new blessings, and new opportunities for me to share the love of Christ and to serve him.

Each day God offers us the opportunity to renew our relationships with our neighbours. What's new? Everything – because every day brings something new and gives us the chance to experience and share God's love in new ways.

Prayer: *Dear Lord, thank you for giving us another day to experience something new. We pray as Jesus taught us, saying, 'Our Father in heaven, hallowed be your name, your kingdom come, your will be done on earth as it is in heaven. Give us today our daily bread. Forgive us our debts, as we also have forgiven our debtors. And lead us not into temptation, but deliver us from the evil one.'* Amen*

Thought for the day: How can I do something new for God and my neighbour today?

Stanislav Ossipov (Tallinn, Estonia)

PRAYER FOCUS: THOSE SEEKING A NEW RELATIONSHIP WITH GOD

*Matthew 6:9–13, NIV

ry ground

Read Joshua 4:1–9

Joshua set up twelve stones in the middle of the Jordan... and they are there to this day.
Joshua 4:9 (NRSV)

Several years ago, my husband and I felt content with our lives. We had five young children, a beautiful home and were both working at jobs we loved. We thanked God regularly for all the good things in our lives. Then my husband was made redundant. This news felt like being punched in the stomach. We lost our home and many of our other belongings. Nearly all our savings had to be used for moving expenses.

I grew up knowing that when trials come, I need to rely more strongly on my faith. So, in this struggle I tried to remember that I serve a God who has never let me down. I made a list of all the ways God had been faithful to my family and me. The blessings seemed endless.

When Joshua placed those twelve stones in the Jordan, they were to serve as a reminder that at one time the ground was dry. God's power provided a dry ground in the middle of a raging river so that Joshua could lead the Israelites through to God's future. After everyone had crossed, and Joshua had set up the pile of twelve stones, the waters crashed in, covering all evidence of their passage, but the stones remained as a solid reminder of God's help for the Israelites. This story can give us the hope and courage to trust God to present new possibilities when our path seems impossible.

Prayer: *Heavenly Father, help us to respond in faith when we face difficulties, and bring to our minds the signs of your never-failing goodness to us. Amen*

Thought for the day: Even in difficult times, I will remember God's faithfulness.

Shontell Brewer (Nevada, US)

New life

Read Ephesians 2:1–10

If anyone is in Christ, there is a new creation: everything old has passed away; see, everything has become new!
2 Corinthians 5:17 (NRSV)

Four years ago, I moved to a new housing estate. In front of each house was a maple tree. I noticed that the tree in front of my house was infested with insects, and one day, during a gale, the tree broke at the damaged spot. I gathered up the branches and cut the remaining trunk to the ground.

A few weeks later I noticed a green shoot coming from the stump. Before autumn arrived, the shoot was more than three feet tall. Today the tree has beautifully formed branches and is at least 18 feet tall.

At times our lives may seem broken beyond repair. Troubles may leave us devastated and hopeless. But we have a God who loves us through our brokenness. His grace can remove the debris in our lives and help us to grow into something even better than before. It may take time, but we can trust that God will help us transform our lives into something strong and beautiful.

Prayer: *Lord Jesus, thank you for healing the brokenness in our lives. Forgive us and transform each of us into the beautiful person you intend us to be. Amen*

Thought for the day: When all seems lost, God can help me rebuild my life.

Lyle Weldon (Kentucky, US)

In God's image

Read Romans 8:26–30

Job said, 'Naked came I out of my mother's womb, and naked shall I return... the Lord gave and the Lord hath taken away; blessed be the name of the Lord.'

Job 1:21 (KJV)

For 40 years, I struggled with a number of issues – from low self-esteem to drug and alcohol abuse – until one day the police came to my door with a search warrant. After turning my house upside down, they led me away in handcuffs. Before I was arrested, I believed in but didn't have a relationship with God. That was about to change.

As I began to read scripture, I also began to see and feel God's love. I had lost most of my family and money and I had damaged my health through my addictions. But God never gave up on me. I went back to my childhood church and was welcomed with more love than I had known in quite a while.

Now it is my turn to care for others. Most days I lead and volunteer with addiction recovery groups, a local homeless shelter, a food bank and various Bible studies. God didn't give up on me. Instead he helped me to become the person I was created to be.

Prayer: *Our Father in heaven, help us to remember that we are always in your loving and trustworthy hands. Strengthen our faith so that we may grow to be more like you. In the name of your Son, Jesus Christ. Amen*

Thought for the day: God never gives up on me.

Jeff Long (North Carolina, US)

A faithful steward

Read 1 Peter 4:8–11

Offer hospitality to one another without grumbling. Each of you should use whatever gift you have received to serve others, as faithful stewards of God's grace in its various forms.

1 Peter 4:9–10 (NIV)

I have the privilege of being a stay-at-home mum to my six children. This allows me to spend time with them during the day, greet them after school, teach them and watch them grow. One of the drawbacks, however, is that my days are full of mundane tasks: washing up, doing laundry, sweeping the floor, changing nappies and tidying toys away. These things are not exciting or fun, but they need to be done.

One day as I was matching socks today's quoted verse came to mind. Do I grumble? Is my work really blessing others if I have a bad attitude? Sometimes it seems that no one else cares about the chores I do, but then I realise, as I sit alone matching piles of socks and folding tiny clothes, that God sees me. God knows my heart and attitude. He knows if I am working as a joyful servant or just trying to cross things off my to-do list.

God notices all of us even in the mundane and seemingly pointless tasks of our daily lives. When we take the opportunity to serve others with love, we are faithful stewards of his grace – no matter how dull the task might be.

Prayer: *Dear God, help us to serve others joyfully as we go about our daily tasks. Thank you for allowing us to be stewards of your grace. Amen*

Thought for the day: Today I will serve God and others with a joyful heart.

Sarah Lyons (Kansas, US)

Reflecting God's love

Read Colossians 3:12–17
As water reflects the face, so one's life reflects the heart.
Proverbs 27:19 (NIV)

My husband and I walked down to the lake, which lay still in the early morning sunshine. Its surface perfectly reflected the world above – hills of dark green fir and pine and a deep blue sky with puffy white clouds floating by. I couldn't even distinguish the actual colour of the water, so bright were the reflections.

If only I could reflect God in such a way! The Bible helps by showing me how to live by Jesus' example. He loved the poor, reached out to help the sick and forgave those who hurt him. But still I ask myself, 'Why is it so hard for me to live the same way?' Perhaps my soul becomes agitated by stress, by guilt over wrongs I have done or by memories of times I've been hurt.

When we find ourselves stumbling over such obstacles, we can allow God to calm these storms by singing songs of praise, praying for forgiveness and focusing on our blessings. As we do so, the inner disturbances subside. We will be more able to reflect the beauty and light of God's love.

Prayer: *Dear Lord, revive us with your Spirit so that we will reflect your love to everyone around us. Amen*

Thought for the day: How can I reflect God's love today?

Susan Thogerson Maas (Oregon, US)

An awesome responsibility

Read Psalm 34:1–8

This poor soul cried, and was heard by the Lord, and was saved from every trouble.
Psalm 34:6 (NRSV)

In March 2003 I had a serious stroke. It was an especially difficult time because I am left-handed and was paralysed on my left side for quite a while. The doctors did not expect me to recover, but God had another plan. I did recover, went back to college and began a new career.

After my stroke, I went through a time when I was obsessed with getting better and wanting to see my sons grow up. I began to feel sorry for myself. But I finally said, 'Lord, only you can take away my fears. I will trust you.'

I look back on that experience often. I don't take life for granted any longer. God loves all of us and wants what is best for us. Now I spend time with God in prayer many times each day. I am thankful for the privilege of prayer, but I also realise that prayer is an awesome responsibility. We all go through difficult situations in life, and some are worse than others. But how we deal with those situations is what is important. If we pray and pray expectantly, our difficulties can turn into blessings as well as great opportunities to encourage and bless others.

Prayer: *Dear Lord, thank you for the privilege and responsibility of prayer. May we use our difficulties as a way to encourage others. In Jesus' name. Amen*

Thought for the day: Today, I am thankful for the privilege of prayer.

Michael Slaton (Alabama, US)

Eyes closing

Read Acts 12:1–6

I lie down and sleep; I wake again, because the Lord sustains me. I will not fear though tens of thousands assail me on every side.
Psalm 3:5-6 (NIV)

Four-year-old James climbed into his car seat, and we drove off. 'My eyes are closing down,' he announced sleepily. No wonder! He had just spent a long day playing on the beach and splashing in the sea.

I laughed. My eyes were also drooping. How easily sleep takes over when we have had plenty of fresh air and exercise. Sleep is one of God's good gifts to us, but sometimes circumstances require us to keep awake a bit longer.

How wonderful that God's eyes never droop! In today's reading, Herod had just killed Peter's friend and planned to have Peter killed the next day. Imprisoned and chained to soldiers, he had good reason to spend a sleepless night. But his eyes drooped and he slept. Even while Peter slept, some stayed awake all night praying for him. He was in the hands of the God who never slumbers or sleeps (see Psalm 121:4, NIV). We can rest, knowing that the same is true for us.

Prayer: *Dear God, we need not fear because you are watching over us. Thank you for your love and constant care. Amen*

Thought for the day: I can close my eyes and rest, knowing that God never sleeps.

Marion Turnbull (Liverpool, England)

Determination

Read John 4:34–36

The thief comes only to steal and kill and destroy; I have come that they may have life, and have it to the full.
John 10:10 (NIV)

I walked out of the nursing home feeling like a failure. I had gone to visit a friend and to tell him about the good news of Jesus. Yet, as usual, I lacked the courage. Over the following weeks, I prayed earnestly for courage to share my faith. I know that this type of evangelism is not everyone's gift, but the opportunity to share the gospel of Jesus and the abundant life he offers has become a passion for me.

After many prayers, the day finally came when I decided I would no longer let my fear stop me. One day soon after, following God's nudging, I approached a man in a cafeteria. Pulse increasing, voice cracking, I asked, 'Have you accepted Jesus as your Lord and Saviour?' With tears, he replied, 'My mum on her death bed asked me to do that.' We prayed, and he asked Jesus into his life.

At times, we may feel as if we have failed God. But when we continue to pray, we will discover opportunities to use the gifts God has given us. When we are willing to serve, he is willing to give us the strength and power to fulfil the plans we have made. Above all, we can come to love doing his will.

Prayer: *Dear God, show us our gifts, and guide us to opportunities to use them. Restore our passion for your work and help us to seek your will above our own. Amen*

Thought for the day: I will pray for courage to answer God's call.

Randy Tramp (South Dakota, US)

Beautiful, broken shells

Read Romans 5:1–11

We... boast in our sufferings, knowing that suffering produces endurance, and endurance produces character, and character produces hope, and hope does not disappoint us, because God's love has been poured into our hearts through the Holy Spirit.

Romans 5:3–5 (NRSV)

When I dig a seashell out of the sand I first turn it one way and then the other to see its condition. Does it have chips or cracks, or is it whole and complete? I am looking for a perfect shell – not a broken one. Often, we are content only with the perfect, the unblemished, the new.

That is not the way with God, who understands the broken, the imperfect and the damaged – and seeks us. The scripture for today shows us that we humans are like the imperfect shell. We journey through an ocean filled with rocks and reefs and storms, and none of us makes it to the shore without scars of suffering and endurance.

At times, we may feel disappointed or ashamed at our brokenness. But in our suffering we are being made strong. And that strength will develop a character that clings to hope. Our hope is not in circumstances, people or even ourselves, but in our powerful and loving God who will never let us be crushed or lost in the storm. God can transform our stories of suffering into a beautiful strength of character that produces hope which will never disappoint.

Prayer: *Dear God, give us strength to withstand the storms we encounter. Help us to cling to you in hope. Amen*

Thought for the day: God can transform my suffering into strength.

Amy B. Trent (California, US)

The missing piece

Read James 4:1–10

I will lie down and fall asleep in peace because you alone, Lord, let me live in safety.
Psalm 4:8 (CEB)

My mother enjoys jigsaw puzzles. She starts with the edges and works inward – slowly bringing order to the chaos of small pieces. The process is challenging but satisfying. One puzzle that she worked on didn't go together properly because each time she got close to finishing a certain part of the picture, a necessary piece was missing.

Life can feel like that incomplete puzzle when we forget to rely on God. We try to build our lives out of the pieces we have: education, money or material goods. Just when things seem to be coming together properly, frustrations creep in. The problem is that we are missing the piece that holds all the other pieces together – God. By coming to God in humble repentance, we receive the grace of our Lord's forgiveness and love.

Following God in service is seldom easy, but it comes with peaceful assurance. He will guide our steps and can cause good to come out of the worst situation. He brings order and peace out of the chaos of life's small pieces.

Prayer: *God of grace, thank you for your promise to deliver us from evil. May your love and mercy guide our actions so we may know your peace each day. Amen*

Thought for the day: God wants me to have true peace.

Gale A. Richards (Iowa, US)

The gift of a Bible

Read Psalm 119:105–112

Your word is a lamp for my feet, a light on my path.
Psalm 119:105 (NIV)

My hand reached for the gift as everyone in the congregation watched. I pulled the book toward me, admiring its big, gold lettering. HOLY BIBLE was stamped across the front. At the time, I didn't realise how precious this gift was.

A few years later, I carried that same Bible as I walked into a small country church. Each Sunday as I read from that Bible, my faith and God's word became real.

It's easy to depend on others to hear God's word, leaving our own Bible closed and untouched. The Bible is personal, a lamp for our path today and for the future. Reading the Bible offers guidance in any stage of life. It encourages us to forgive, to find hope and to love others.

My gift from a thoughtful congregation when I was a student going to college has served me well for nearly 30 years. Its pages – some of them now crumpled from years of use – contain many handwritten notes of insight and guidance. Its words have provided powerful wisdom to lead me through these 30 years. God's word is truly a lamp for life's path, a gift given to each of us.

Prayer: *Dear God, thank you for the Bible and your guidance through it. May its words become an even brighter lamp, guiding us every day. Amen*

Thought for the day: I will seek guidance from the Bible today.

Kristi Woods (Oklahoma, US)

Always with us

Read Romans 8:31–39

[The Lord your God] will never leave you nor forsake you.
Deuteronomy 31:6 (NIV)

As a 20-year-old Bible college graduate, I kissed my parents goodbye and went to teach the Bible in south-east Asia. I had planned the whole adventure on my own and was travelling by myself for the entire summer. I was thrilled – that is, until my first day in the country when I found myself sitting cross-legged on a cold tile floor with my back against a wall. Far from anything familiar and with no one to talk to, I felt deeply and utterly alone.

Sometimes we force our own backs against a wall; at other times life pushes us there. We may be anxious, depressed, afraid for the future or lonely. We know we can't backtrack, but the way ahead looks murky.

I imagine David feeling this way when he wrote, 'I walk through the darkest valley' (Psalm 23:4, NIV). Yet he was careful to add: 'I will fear no evil, for you are with me.' When our backs are against the wall, we can look to our heavenly Father for peace. Like David, when we focus not on the darkness but on God's goodness, we can find comfort. That day, I sang in worship to God.

Someone else might have quoted scripture or prayed. However, we respond, we can trust that God is always with us, leading us through the darkness.

Prayer: *Dear Father God, thank you for comforting us with your words in scripture that remind us of your faithful presence. Amen*

Thought for the day: I am never alone because God is with me.

Samuel Hunt (Florida, US)

Flooded with light

Read Ephesians 1:15–23

I pray that the eyes of your heart may be enlightened in order that you may know the hope to which [God] has called you, the riches of his glorious inheritance in his holy people.
Ephesians 1:18 (NIV)

Rainy days give me a slow, sleepy kind of feeling. While I usually enjoy these days, sometimes even when I seem to have no reason to feel sad, I feel dreary. Then the sun peeks out, and suddenly I feel warm and cheerful again. The light from the sun honestly changes my mood. The New Living Translation of the Bible says 'I pray that your hearts will be flooded with light' instead of using 'enlightened' in the verse from Ephesians above.

When our hearts are flooded with God's light through scripture, we can feel the warmth and peace he offers. God loves us and cares for us all the days of our lives. Just as the sun's light changed my mood from dreary to happy, so scripture can change our minds and hearts from being cloudy and uncertain to being confident in God's presence and peace. No matter what the day may bring, his light brightens our lives.

Prayer: *O God, illumine our minds and hearts with your words so that we may gain a better understanding of you and your will for our lives. Amen*

Thought for the day: Even on cloudy days, the light of God's love is shining.

Margie J. Harding (Maryland, US)

Robin's nest

Read Acts 2:41–42
You and I may be mutually encouraged by each other's faith.
Romans 1:12 (NIV)

Pamela met me at the chapel door, her face bright with eagerness as she showed me the shoebox in her hands. It was full of dried grass and moss and some shreds of paper. 'I've made a nest,' she said. 'A robin will come to live in it!'

How could I explain to a young child so full of faith that a robin will usually build its own nest and might prefer a round one? Reflecting on this experience led me to another important truth. Pamela could offer all the materials for a nest, but the robin had to build it herself. In the same way, we may also find ourselves wanting to build other people's faith for them. But we forget that our Christian experiences are unique because each is between us and our Lord. Our lives are bound together in fellowship and built on the same materials of faith and love. Today's verse reminds us to share our faith and the love of Christ with one another as we each build our own relationship with God.

Prayer: *Dear Father, you have given us this life in Christ to enjoy and to share. Help us to support one another as we build our relationships with you. Amen*

Thought for the day: How am I building my own relationship with Christ?

Colin D. Harbach (Cumbria, England)

To give and receive

Read Galatians 6:9–10

Give, and it will be given to you. A good measure, pressed down, shaken together and running over, will be poured into your lap. For with the measure you use, it will be measured to you.
Luke 6:38 (NIV)

My husband, John, is a window cleaner and was finishing his last job before a holiday weekend. Then I got a call from him. 'I need you to come and get me. I've fallen and I'm hurt.'

In the hospital we talked about our faith in God. We began to plan how we would survive, since his business provided our family's sole income. We listed the small luxuries we could give up and recounted all the blessings that remained. Doctors confirmed that John had crushed his heel bone. Surgery and a long recovery lay ahead, with no guarantee of returning to work. Although the future was uncertain, our trust remained.

In the weeks that followed, God taught us how to receive. Our church members generously paid our bills. Some of our customers paid us even though we could not work for them.

Many of us are devoted to looking for ways to give, but for some the more challenging lesson is to receive. We may be troubled by doubts of whether we are worthy of the gift or we feel as if we should repay it in some way. But receiving gifts with no strings attached teaches us about God's grace. We cannot earn it and we cannot repay it. We can only receive that grace – which is the essence of the gospel.

Prayer: *Dear God help us to be generous in giving and gracious in receiving. Amen*

Thought for the day: God calls us to give and teaches us to receive.

Katherine Rice (Oregon, US)

Brain break

Read Psalm 121:1–8

I lift up my eyes to the hills – from where will my help come? My help comes from the Lord.
Psalm 121:1–2 (NRSV)

My announcement of, 'Brain break!' always brings relief and joy to my pupils. As a teacher, I have found that 13-year-olds are unable to sit through 70 minutes of even my most engaging science lessons. They need a break! A two-minute brain break gives them the opportunity to get out of their seats, stretch or walk across the classroom to chat briefly with a friend. When the teaching begins again, the students are relaxed, refreshed and ready to learn more.

I have found that a brain break can also provide me with some much-needed relief during a long stressful day. I can give myself a few minutes of peace by moving to a quiet place where I can pray, read a passage of scripture or simply rest in God's comforting presence.

A couple of minutes alone with God in the middle of a hectic day might be enough to help us feel spiritually restored, physically revital-ised, and ready to move on. When we feel stressed and overwhelmed, we can take a brain break – some time apart with God.

Prayer: *Thank you, God, for the peace and comfort you bring us even on our most stressful days. Amen*

Thought for the day: Spending time with God can bring me peace.

Jill Allen Maisch (Maryland, US)

Forgiven

Read Luke 15:11–32

While he was still a long way off, his father saw him and was filled with compassion for him; he ran to his son, threw his arms around him and kissed him.

Luke 15:20 (NIV)

I have been in the prodigal son's shoes. I have experienced moments of regret and remorse and have humbly stumbled home. When reading this parable, I have always paid more attention to the prodigal son and have missed the wonderful, life-changing focus of the passage: God's love. Just like the father in this parable, our heavenly Father has a deep love for each of us. God is looking down the road, squinting and scanning the horizon. And when he sees a heart turn or a child stumbling home, he doesn't wait. Like this father, God runs toward each broken child. Each of us is wrapped in love as he welcomes us home. There is no lecture, no scolding, no penance. There is only the perfect and unconditional love of the Father.

When we recognise and accept God's love, we do not have to live in sorrow, shame or regret about our past. Instead, we can share in the prodigal son's relief and live in God's love.

Prayer: *Dear Father, help us to know that we are forgiven and help us to receive your love. Amen*

Thought for the day: Today, I will not allow my past to block my view of God's love.

Stephen Johnson (California, US)

Heal me – now!

Read Psalm 62:5–8

Trust in him at all times, you people; pour out your hearts to him, for God is our refuge.

Psalm 62:8 (NIV)

The emotional pain I felt after my husband and I separated seemed unbearable. We had been married for only two-and-a-half years but had been friends for more than half our lives. I had believed this man to be the love of my life – the person God had chosen for me and me for him. And I was losing him. I was inconsolable.

Days of hurting turned into months. As people around me continued with their lives, I wondered when I would be able to continue with mine. I wanted to feel better now, not in two months or a year. I filled every second of my time, trying to ignore my grief and loneliness. Although many people told me, 'Healing takes time', time felt like the enemy – taunting me because I was losing days and months to my pain and heartache.

But God led me to the verse quoted above, helping me to see that in my yearning to heal quickly, I had forgotten his presence with me even in times of trouble. God had been working on me through each second of my hurt. While I had felt encouraged to pour out my pain to him, I also began to trust that he was giving me the time I needed to grieve and heal properly. The Lord, our refuge, has promised to give us peace and solace, and we can rely on that promise.

Prayer: *Dear Lord, help us to trust you to walk beside us through times of pain and loss. Heal us and restore peace in us. Amen*

Thought for the day: Healing may come slowly, but God is with me through it all.

Jennifer Brigandi (Ontario, Canada)

'I will!'

Read Matthew 28:16–20

Then I heard the voice of the Lord saying, 'Whom shall I send, and who will go for us?' And I said, 'Here am I; send me!'
Isaiah 6:8 (NRSV)

We are a small church community in a beautiful area of the state of New York. Daily we see God's handiwork in glorious hillsides and beautiful lakes and streams. This beauty is an inspiration for us in our ministry of making new disciples of Jesus Christ.

Recently, I invited church members to volunteer to lead one of several planned ministry events. I was reading out the list of ministries when suddenly I heard an enthusiastic 'I will!' Everyone cheered! I looked up to see who had volunteered. To my delight, the very first volunteer was Ella, an eleven-year-old girl.

That ministry was to lead a social evening as a way of reaching out to the local community. Ella's enthusiasm and energy in taking on such a key role reminded me that Jesus has commanded us to be eager to serve and to be as humble as a child in sharing the love of Christ. Our eagerness to serve others shows the joy of the Lord in our lives, and that joy draws others to Jesus.

Prayer: *Thank you, Lord, for the excitement of young people in the church. May we be inspired by their spirit to share your love with others. Amen*

Thought for the day: How can I invite others to join me in serving God?

Vincent W. Howell (New York, US)

Smooth sailing

Read James 5:13–16

Every word of God is flawless; he is a shield to those who take refuge in him.
Proverbs 30:5 (NIV)

Within hours of sailing, every cruise ship requires all travellers to report on deck for a muster drill. The crew instructs passengers about the location of the lifeboats, which ones to board, where life jackets can be found, and how to put them on correctly. This knowledge is shared as a safeguard, in case of an emergency.

Through the years, I've become aware of other lifesavers that keep me afloat during daily crises. A network of fellow believers – church, family and friends – lift me in prayer when I feel myself drowning in troubles. I trust a smaller circle of confidantes for thoughtful counsel when I need direction (Proverbs 27:9). And during desperate times, when my faith is lost in a fog of worries or depression, no life jacket fits as securely as the eternal, unconditional support of God's word. Immersing myself in scripture keeps me from sinking. I can rejoice in the Bible's life-saving power and the wisdom held between its covers, knowing that I am prepared.

Prayer: *Dear God, lift us up with your word. Inspire us to reach out to others through prayer and loving service as we pray, 'Father, hallowed be your name, your kingdom come. Give us each day our daily bread. Forgive us our sins, for we also forgive everyone who sins against us. And lead us not into temptation.'* Amen

Thought for the day: Which Bible verses are my lifesavers?

Heidi Gaul (Oregon, US)

Splinters

Read Matthew 11:28–30

Jesus said, 'Come unto me, all ye that labour and are heavy laden, and I will give you rest.'
Matthew 11:28 (KJV)

One day, after doing some DIY, I discovered a splinter in each of my thumbs. At first they did not bother me. After all, five minutes with a needle, a little disinfectant, and the problem would be solved! In the evening, I began the procedure. But I was not able to pull the splinters out. I tried again the next day and the next but could not remove them. After these failures, I decided to go to the internet. Reading others' experiences introduced me to many interesting ways to extract splinters, from honey to a banana peel. But none worked for me. On the third morning, when my thumbs began to swell and became very painful, I decided to see a doctor.

While I waited for an experienced nurse to rid me of the painful splinters, I prayed and pondered how deeply ingrained in human nature is the desire to do everything without asking for help. What's worse, when it comes to spiritual pain, we sometimes get so tired of trying to get rid of certain 'splinters' on our own that we give up.

The truth is that we can't improve our spiritual condition by ourselves. But when we overcome our arrogance and give our burdens to the Lord, we can find relief. Our pain will be resolved as we become closer to our creator.

Prayer: *Physician of our souls, heal us from the splinters of sin so that we may be healthy in body, soul and spirit. In Jesus' name. Amen*

Thought for the day: What 'splinter' prevents me from focusing on God today?

Stanislav Prokhorov (Samara, Russia)

Stiff-necked people

Read Deuteronomy 10:14–22

Circumcise your hearts, therefore, and do not be stiff-necked any longer.

Deuteronomy 10:16 (NIV)

'Stiff-necked'. I smile at this description of the disobedient, stubborn Israelites because thanks to a pet calf, I know exactly what 'stiff-necked' means. When I was a young girl growing up on a dairy farm, calves were my playmates. I particularly loved the beautiful brown Jersey calves that looked like deer.

One day I decided to put a halter on Ginger, my favourite calf, so I could lead her around the farm and perhaps even take her to the fair. I slipped the halter strap over her head with ease, but when I pulled on it, she did not follow. The more I tugged, the more she planted her feet and stiffened her neck. After several minutes of battling wills, Ginger and I both became tired and sat on the ground. Her refusal to follow me meant she had to stay in the field, and I couldn't take her to the fair.

I sometimes picture myself as a stiff-necked calf digging in my heels, refusing to be led by God, and missing out on a fulfilling relationship. But God has more patience with me than I had with Ginger. Thankfully, he never gives up on stiff-necked people like me.

Prayer: *Dear God, help us not to be stiff-necked and to follow you and your goodness all the days of our lives. Amen*

Thought for the day: Where is God leading me?

Terry Cobb (Missouri, US)

Our refuge and strength

Read Isaiah 41:8–13

The Lord says, 'When you pass through the waters, I will be with you; when through the rivers, they won't sweep over you... Look! I'm doing a new thing; now it sprouts up.'
Isaiah 43:2, 19 (CEB)

Where I live, the water department sometimes randomly cuts off the water supply. One day, I decided to store extra water before it was cut off again. I turned on the tap to fill the bath. I knew I had to turn it off before I left for work, but in all the hubbub of the day, I forgot. Later, I received a call from my husband, Jorge, telling me that the house was flooded! For the first time, I experienced the fear and pain of such a disaster. I was responsible for what had happened and was angry with myself. But Jorge was sympathetic. He told me not to worry and that with God's help everything would be all right. Placing my trust in God, I prayed for strength.

Weeks later, I was moved to share this experience with other *Upper Room* readers. I wanted to encourage others whose homes have been affected by sudden floods or who feel overwhelmed with problems. As God calmed the waters that devastated my life, he will do the same for all who cry out in prayer. Though we may be responsible for some accidents, as I was, we can trust in the promise that God will always be by our side and will not let us be swept away.

Prayer: *Loving God, help us remember not to be discouraged or afraid, for you will sustain us with your strong hand. Amen*

Thought for the day: 'God is our refuge and strength' (Psalm 46:1, CEB).

Priscilla Morales (Puerto Rico)

Allegiance to Christ

Read Philippians 3:17—4:1

[God] brought [Abram] outside and said, 'Look toward heaven and count the stars, if you are able to count them.' Then he said to him, 'So shall your descendants be.'

Genesis 15:5 (NRSV)

When visiting a church in Missouri, I was surprised to see miniature flags representing nations from all over the world displayed inside. The colourful flags from countries including Mexico, Poland, South Korea, Greece, Nepal, and Kenya provided a helpful, visual reminder that our Christian faith ultimately connects us across barriers of language, ethnicity and national allegiances.

In Genesis 15 we read that Abram was told he would be the father of many nations. Later, the apostle Paul wrote, 'Our citizenship is in heaven, and it is from there that we are expecting a Saviour, the Lord Jesus Christ' (Philippians 3:20, NRSV). Through him we gain access to God's eternal kingdom.

On Sunday mornings, I recall that display of flags from many nations. So, as I sing, pray and bring gifts to God, I remember that we all are brothers and sisters in Christ.

Prayer: *Dear God, make us aware of the needs of Christians around the world, and help us to respond generously. Amen*

Thought for the day: Our ultimate allegiance is to Christ.

David W. Poe (Missouri, US)

Eager to serve

Read Acts 8:26–40
Faith by itself, if it has no works, is dead.
James 2:17 (NRSV)

My friend Sheila was asked to help at a church function. So, one wet and windy evening she made a considerable effort to be at the church. But when she arrived, she found she was not needed, so she started her journey back home.

A man sitting in front of her on the bus turned around and said, 'I'm going to ask J.C. to stop this rain.' Sheila quickly replied, 'I think Jesus Christ is more interested in your soul.' They got off the bus at the same stop and continued their conversation.

Sheila gently explained the love, sacrifice and redemption offered by the One whose name the man had taken so lightly. It turned out that Sheila was just where God wanted her to be.

Sheila's story reminds me of Philip in today's reading. He was where God needed him to be at a particular time. Philip was ready to follow where God led him and was eager to share the scriptures and his faith.

Only God knows when and where we will have the opportunity to share his love and power. Our job is to be ready to follow the promptings of the Holy Spirit as we share our faith.

Prayer: *Heavenly Father, help us know when to speak and act as we share your love with others. Amen*

Thought for the day: How is God leading me to share my faith today?

Carol Purves (Cumbria, England)

Not forgotten

Read Isaiah 49:13–18

Can a mother forget the baby at her breast and have no compassion on the child she has borne? Though she may forget, I will not forget you! See, I have engraved you on the palms of my hands.

Isaiah 49:15–16 (NIV)

A few years ago, as my mother started to suffer from dementia, I lived with her and served as her carer. Even though she was forgetting many things, she retained old memories including the names of her nine children. She still recognised family members and knew me most of the time. However, there were instances when she would call me by another name or think I was someone else.

The first time she called me by my cousin's name I thought my name had just slipped her mind. However, she began to call me by my cousin's name when asking other family members about me when I was away from home. One time she asked me, 'How is your mother?' I was stunned and could not answer. Another time, my mother asked my older sister, 'Who is this woman who lives with me?'

Watching my mother lose her mental capacities was a painful experience that made me feel abandoned and forgotten. But then I realised that at times we all feel that way. When I feel forgotten, I take comfort in today's quoted scripture verses, knowing that God does not forget my mother or me. Through our relationship with Jesus, God knows each of our names.

Prayer: *Dear Lord, when we feel forgotten and abandoned, help us remember your great love for us. In Jesus' name we pray. Amen*

Thought for the day: God will never forget me.

Maria Victoria P. Creel (Alabama, US)

The great commission

Read Matthew 28:16–20
Go into all the world and preach the gospel to all creation.
Mark 16:15 (NIV)

My wife and I sit in our conservatory every morning and watch the birds feed at our strategically placed birdfeeders. One day I noticed a bird that had the brightest red colour on his body, but most of the red was covered by his wings. You could see the bright red feathers only when he spread his wings to fly. When he sat still, he looked like just another bird.

That made me think. When I, as a Christian, stand still and do not follow God's call, I am just another person living in a sinful world. By not inviting others to join my church family, I fail to show the world the wonderful fellowship that God inspires in believers. In today's reading, Jesus told his disciples to go and proclaim the gospel throughout the world. This same commandment applies to all of us. God created birds to fly and us to glorify him and spread the good news. Living in this way brings out the beauty and the best in each of us.

Prayer: *Dear Father, help us to glorify you and spread your good news to the world. Amen*

Thought for the day: How can I create beauty today by sharing the good news of Jesus?

Charles 'Greg' Eary (West Virginia, US)

Hidden from view

Read Deuteronomy 31:1–8

The Lord himself goes before you and will be with you; he will never leave you nor forsake you. Do not be afraid; do not be discouraged.
Deuteronomy 31:8 (NIV)

At our home in Oregon, we keep an umbrella by our door because we get such heavy rain from October to April that we can go for days without seeing the sun, moon or stars. Although these sources of light may be hidden by the clouds and rain, we know they are still in the heavens.

It is harder to find assurance that there is still light when we encounter 'clouds' like death, disease, depression and war. It can feel as though God is hiding or ignoring us. Where is the assurance that he is still there and cares about our problems?

When I feel separated from God by the 'clouds' of my life, I turn to his promises in the Bible for reassurance. Jesus promises to be with us 'to the very end of the age' (Matthew 28:20). The psalmist declares that God 'who watches over Israel will neither slumber nor sleep' (Psalm 121:4). And scripture assures us that God's presence is everywhere.

Reading the Bible every day and memorising verses about God's presence can act as an umbrella in the rain. When clouds of fear appear, we can remember and repeat these biblical promises. Holding on to God's word can shelter us from fear and help our faith to grow.

Prayer: *Dear God, thank you for keeping us constantly in your care. Amen*

Thought for the day: Scripture can be an umbrella in every storm life brings.

Jane Reid (Oregon, US)

Accepting help

Read Exodus 14:9–18
The Lord will fight for you; you need only to be still.
Exodus 14:14 (NIV)

One morning on holiday, my daughter and I took a walk along the beach. We saw a small crab sidling quickly toward the water. But the tide was coming in, and for every inch it progressed, a wave would hit the shore, causing the crab to somersault further back along the sand. After each wave, the crab would right itself and resume its journey toward the water, undaunted. Soon, a small group had gathered to watch this crab. We were all sympathetic, knowing that the struggle was in vain – that eventually the crab would exhaust itself and be stranded on the beach, food for seagulls.

One man grabbed a stick, hoping the crab would latch on so that he could toss it into the sea. But to the crab the stick appeared threatening, and it immediately threw up its little pincers, ready to fight. The tiny crab looked so silly trying to fight this big man. Finally, a teenage boy dumped sand on the crab to stop it fighting, scooped it up in a big mound of sand, and placed it into the sea. How much like this crab I am! How I fight when God sends help! I seem almost determined to struggle, as if I know what's best. But when our efforts fail, we can remember to put our trust in God alone, who places us gently where we belong.

Prayer: *Dear God, help us to recognise when we are relying solely on ourselves, and turn us back to you. Amen*

Thought for the day: God calls me to accept the help that others offer.

Carolyn Chapman (Missouri, US)

Clarence

Read James 2:14–18

Since there will never cease to be some in need on the earth, I therefore command you, 'Open your hand to the poor and needy neighbour in your land.'
Deuteronomy 15:11 (NRSV)

After the service in the small rural church, the two dozen worshippers moved into an adjoining room for coffee and biscuits. Although I was a visitor, I knew one man by reputation. Many of my meals-on-wheels recipients spoke glowingly of Clarence, a man who volunteers with others in the church to deliver non-perishable food and other necessities to them when their need is great but funds are low.

I watched 80-year-old Clarence move briskly about the room, and once he settled at a table I joined him. When I expressed my admiration and gratitude for what he did in the community, he shrugged. 'I'm just an old man, but I hope to keep doing this for a while. Maybe I'll retire when I'm 90.'

Regardless of age, few of us can match the stamina and giving spirit of Clarence, but we can all watch for opportunities to show God's love to others. Whatever we do for others in the name of Jesus – a prayer, a kind word, an offer to assist with a simple task, a gift from our garden – is pleasing to God.

Prayer: *Gracious God, help us to recognise ways in which we can serve others in our community. Amen*

Thought for the day: I will do what I can, then trust God to do the rest.

Robert E. Boertien (Oregon, US)

Troubling times

Read Psalm 23:1–6

Don't judge, so that you won't be judged. You'll receive the same judgment you give.
Matthew 7:1–2 (CEB)

In 2005 I was unjustly sacked from my job. For 14 months I remained at home, waiting, while my legal case was under review. Each morning I woke up anxious and sad, praying that my name would be cleared and that justice would be done. However, as the days passed, this disquieting experience became, in fact, a positive one for me.

During those 14 months, I was able to be with my grandmother and great-aunt, to spend time with them and care for them. And from them I learned the important lessons demonstrated in their daily devotional time, the spiritual depth of their unshakable faith in God, and the power and strength of prayer. In the end, my case was resolved. I resumed my position as director at my college, and I was warmly received again.

The following year my wonderful grandmother died; the next year so did my beloved aunt. Their painful absence has been lessened by the memory of the time I spent with them and their witness and example of faithful living and prayer. My time with them restored my faith and left no doubt that God was at work to deliver me from an injustice.

Prayer: *Almighty God, we are grateful that you are always ready to attend to our needs in the most difficult situations. Amen*

Thought for the day: God always works for good.

Edio E. García Galleguillos (Coquimbo, Chile)

At the pizza counter

Read 2 Corinthians 13:5–13

Brothers and sisters, rejoice! Strive for full restoration, encourage one another, be of one mind, live in peace. And the God of love and peace will be with you.
2 Corinthians 13:11 (NIV)

When I arrived at the supermarket to pick up the pizzas for our fund-raising event, I was already running late. I had just finished officiating at a wedding 40 miles away and was rushing to get back on time. The queue at the pizza counter was long and, once I got closer, I realised why. There stood a frazzled mother, along with her children, paying for her entire trolley full of purchases at the pizza counter! As I stood there fuming, no one else seemed to be bothered. Even the assistant seemed to be joyful as he scanned her numerous items.

I realised then that I was allowing something very small to take over my spirit. Yes, it was inconvenient to have to stand there for an extra five minutes, but the end result was a less-frazzled mother with one fewer stops to make on her way out of the supermarket.

Doesn't God treat us with the same patience – standing by while we work things out? He doesn't huff and puff when we take our time. So why couldn't I offer that woman the same grace I am given?

I pray that I will learn to take a moment to be joyful and thankful for all things, and to learn to slow down and take it all in. Every moment – even a frustrating moment waiting at a pizza counter – is sacred.

Prayer: *Dear God, help us to extend grace to everyone we meet. Help us to be the light you created us to be. Amen*

Thought for the day: Even in times of stress and frustration, I can extend grace to others.

Crystal Senter-Brown (Massachusetts, US)

True wealth

Read Luke 16:1–13

No one can serve two masters. Either you will hate the one and love the other, or you will be devoted to the one and despise the other. You cannot serve both God and money.
Luke 16:13 (NIV)

When I was young, I wanted to be a pop star because I wanted fame and money. For as long as I could remember, my mother and I had been surviving by visiting food banks, and I could not imagine living the rest of my life with this shame that hung over me daily like a raincloud.

At the age of 34, I found myself drowning in a sea of whisky and sinking to the bottom without any money in my pocket. My intense desire for wealth had controlled me and nearly killed me. I begged God to pull me out of this situation. After all, the Bible says that God is always with us. And he heard my cry and rescued me.

For nearly four years I have been sober – thanks to my heavenly Father. Turning my back on the idol of money, I made the decision to serve my Master – something I was utterly unable to do when my focus was on trying to become rich. It took many years and much struggling, but because of my decision to follow and serve God, I have received more peace, love and life than I ever dreamed possible. And this is true wealth.

Prayer: *Dear Lord, help us to remember that neither money nor any other worldly possession can fill our souls like you can. Amen*

Thought for the day: God is always with me.

Sabrina Nicodemus (Ohio, US)

What's in a name?

Read 2 Chronicles 3:1–17

[Solomon] set up the pillars in front of the temple, one on the right, the other on the left; the one on the right he called Jachin, and the one on the left, Boaz.
2 Chronicles 3:17 (NRSV)

When my wife and I were in England a few years ago, we noticed that nearly every house had a name posted on the outside. We had rented a 15th-century house called The Old Manor House. Next door was another old house called The Manor House. Up the road was The Abbey, with The Manse across the street.

We had just built a new home and joked about giving it a name: 'Home, Sweet Home: Better Than We Thought' was appropriate – but a bit wordy! 'Biggest Cheque We Ever Wrote' was accurate – but somewhat crass!

As our reading describes, when people entered the temple precincts their attention would have been drawn to Jachin and Boaz, two massive pillars in front of the temple. In Hebrew Jachin means 'He establishes', and Boaz means 'In God is strength'. These two names teach us that when God does the building, when his plans are honoured and followed, he will help see them through to completion.

When we have plans that need God's help, we can look to him as visitors to the temple would have those two pillars. If our plans truly reside within God's will, he will surely establish them and give us the strength to complete them.

Prayer: *Dear Lord, in the name of Jesus, we pray for your will to be done in our lives. Amen*

Thought for the day: God will establish and strengthen us as we serve others in love.

John A. Fischer (Washington, US)

Red-shirt Saturday

Read 1 Corinthians 13:1–13

We love because [God] first loved us.
1 John 4:19 (NIV)

My colleague John spends most Saturdays with his grandson, Carson. They wear matching red shirts for their fun adventures and work days together. The relationship is filled with love, trust, caring and joy. Recently, John celebrated his birthday with his family. After he had blown out the candles on the cake, Carson asked him what he wished for. John replied that he didn't make a wish and then asked Carson what he would wish for on his birthday. Carson told John that he would wish for red-shirt Saturdays for the rest of his life!

Carson's reply touched my heart. I thought about my own parents and siblings; my husband, children and grandchildren, and the relationships we share – sometimes loving and wonderful and sometimes not. We learn about love through our human relationships, but we learn about perfect love through our relationship with God. We love because God first loved us. His arms invite each of us in – at any time and at any place.

Following God's will and Jesus' example of loving actions will lead us into relationships that bring satisfaction and joy as well as drawing others to the kingdom of heaven – which is even better than red-shirt Saturday!

Prayer: *Loving Father, thank you for your Son who shows us perfect love. Strengthen and renew us each day so we can love others in his name. Amen*

Thought for the day: We can share with others the love God shows to us.

Kay Hawk (Ohio, US)

A joyful heart

Read 1 Thessalonians 5:12–18
Rejoice always.
1 Thessalonians 5:16 (NIV)

Since I have no car or motorbike, I often walk 30 minutes to church. One day, one of my friends said, 'The distance is so far; don't you get tired?' With a smile, I answered him, 'No, because I do not walk alone. My sister is with me, and we walk with joy.' Our conversation reminded me of when Jesus would have to walk from one place to another to teach and serve large crowds. He didn't let the long distances discourage him from serving with joy. When we do all things with a joyful heart of faith, we will have enough strength even when what we do is very difficult.

Because my sister and I have that same joy, we are happy and enjoy every step of our walk. No matter what trials God's people face, we never tire of living the Christian life because we know that Jesus is walking with us and will never forsake us.

Prayer: *Thank you, God, for giving us strength. Help us to face every trial with joyful hearts because we know that you are always with us. As Jesus taught us, we pray, 'Our Father which art in heaven, Hallowed be thy name. Thy kingdom come. Thy will be done in earth, as it is in heaven. Give us this day our daily bread. And forgive us our debts, as we forgive our debtors. And lead us not into temptation, but deliver us from evil: For thine is the kingdom, and the power, and the glory, for ever. Amen'**

Thought for the day: I can find joy in every circumstance because Jesus is with me.

Meliana Santoso (East Java, Indonesia)

The first step

Read Luke 5:1–11
Simon answered [Jesus], 'Master, we've worked hard all night and haven't caught anything. But because you say so, I will let down the nets.'
Luke 5:5 (NIV)

Simon Peter had spent the entire night fishing with no results when Jesus approached him and told him to get back into his boat and put his nets out in deep water. Fishing was Peter's job, and he had just had a bad night at work. He was probably tired and frustrated, and now here came somebody, who wasn't even a fisherman, telling him how to fish – on the very waters where he had just spent the whole night without catching anything. Peter could have ignored Jesus; he could have shouted an angry response; he could have come up with a dozen reasons to say no. But instead he did what Jesus asked him to do.

Peter not only ended up with a net full of fish, but he took his first step toward a life of incredible faith, a life where he began to fish for people. When we receive an opportunity to serve the Lord, sometimes it may feel as if the opportunity is beyond our abilities. Or perhaps our first reaction may be that it doesn't make sense for us. But listening for God's direction and then following to serve in faith, even when we initially have doubts, is how we grow as followers of Christ.

Prayer: *God, our Guide, give us hearts to listen and wisdom to discern your calling to us. In Jesus' name we pray. Amen*

Thought for the day: In what new way is God calling me to serve?

John D. Bown (Minnesota, US)

You're so strong

Read Psalm 46:1–11

God is our refuge and strength, a very present help in trouble.
Psalm 46:1 (KJV)

On the evening of 28 August 2015, my life as I knew it was forever changed. I watched in panic as Steve, my husband of almost 44 years, took his final breaths on earth.

I was in shock. Most of our friends tried their best to share comforting words. I could only nod half-heartedly. Many people said, 'You are so strong.' I wanted to scream at them, because I had never felt so weak, lonely and vulnerable. I felt rejected and unloved by God. I wondered what I had done to displease God so much that I would lose Steve. How could people call me 'so strong'? I was barely getting through the days and nights I now spent alone. Then God spoke to me. It was not an audible voice, but a very clear thought: 'I will always be with you.'

Even though I miss Steve terribly, I must get up every morning and begin the day God has set before me. I still do not like my 'new normal', but I know that God is with me and has plans for me. He is a very present help in my time of trouble, and he is all I need to go on.

Prayer: *Dear Lord, in times of fear, doubt and questioning, give us the strength to continue to do your will. Amen*

Thought for the day: I can do all things through Christ who strengthens me (see Philippians 4:13).

Beverly Slagle (West Virginia, US)

PRAYER FOCUS: SOMEONE GRIEVING THE LOSS OF A SPOUSE

Ash Wednesday

Read Matthew 1:1–6, 16–17
Salmon was the father of Boaz, whose mother was Rahab.
Matthew 1:5 (CEB)

Whenever I feel that I'm not educated enough, experienced enough or generally not worthy or good enough, I think about the verse quoted above.

The beginning of the book of Matthew contains the lineage of Jesus: 'Salmon was the father of Boaz, whose mother was Rahab.' Only four women are mentioned by name in this lineage. So why is she one of them? Joshua 2:1–14 tells her story.

Rahab was a prostitute. She also hid Hebrew spies and helped them escape in exchange for the lives of her family. I really doubt that Rahab ever felt good enough when she was around the 'religious people', and yet she became an ancestor of Jesus Christ, the Saviour of the world.

I think Rahab was mentioned by name in the book of Matthew for any of us who feel unworthy. God knows our hearts and our insecurities. And Rahab's story shows us that no matter who we are or where we are in life, if we obey, God can use us in amazing ways. As we read the Bible and remain faithful in prayer, he will direct our lives and give us purpose. Because he loves us, we are worthy!

Prayer: *Dear God, thank you for the story of Rahab and for always considering us good enough. Amen*

Thought for the day: Because of God's love, I am worthy and good enough.

Shannon Hurley (Kansas, US)

River of God's love

Read Ezekiel 47:1–12

Wherever the river goes, every living creature that swarms will live, and there will be very many fish, once these waters reach there.
Ezekiel 47:9 (NRSV)

I once stood in the middle of the Mississippi River. I was on holiday north of Itasca, Minnesota, and I stood on a log that spanned the few feet from bank to bank over what was only a small stream. As we continued our trip, we stopped in St Cloud, Minnesota, where the same river is a wide, smooth stream. When we continued south, about halfway down the country, the Mississippi became a mighty, fast-flowing river, at least a mile across.

The Mississippi is like the river in today's reading and quoted scripture verse. The river that Ezekiel walked in, which flowed out of the temple, started small and got deeper and deeper until Ezekiel couldn't cross it. The river watered the trees and nourished the plants and animals.

The way we experience God's love can be like this river. It may begin as just a trickle in our hearts, but it can grow and grow within us until it can't be stopped. We can depend on it for spiritual sustenance. Whenever I remember the holiday I spent down the Mississippi River, I have a renewed assurance of God's power in our lives.

Prayer: *Dear Lord, let us never forget the power of your word that flows into our hearts, feeding and renewing us every day. In Jesus' name. Amen*

Thought for the day: God's love is like a mighty river that nourishes my spirit.

Ken Claar (Idaho, US)

Bread of life

Read Psalm 111:1–10

Jesus said to [the crowd], 'I am the bread of life. Whoever comes to me will never be hungry, and whoever believes in me will never be thirsty.'
John 6:35 (NRSV)

In our small, rural county foodbanks are opening up in many towns, supported by local churches. One church set an example of meeting the needs of children who qualify for free school lunches by giving them with ready-to-eat items to take home for the weekend.

To support this ministry, I review supermarket offers each week, watching for reductions on non-perishable food items. Then I purchase several for the foodbank. I also place my purchases in paper bags so that I can pass the bags on to Sunday school children to decorate. The bags are then given to the foodbank and reused for giving out food and non-perishables to those in need. In this way, the children's artwork becomes an invitation to attend Sunday school and gives the Sunday school children an opportunity to experience mission work.

One individual alone cannot save the world from hunger, but as we give what we can God will multiply our contributions so that more children can be fed.

Prayer: *Dear Jesus, thank you for helping us to provide nourishment to others. Amen*

Thought for the day: When I serve others, God can multiply my efforts.

Rogene McPherson (Kansas, US)

Crying out to the Lord

Read 1 Samuel 26:1–12

I waited patiently for the Lord; he inclined to me and heard my cry.
Psalm 40:1 (NRSV)

Scripture is filled with people who faced dangers and trials. What was it like for David when he was in the wilderness, fleeing from Saul? Perhaps David was as overwhelmed and frightened as I felt when our eldest son, Steven, was diagnosed with leukaemia. Throughout my son's illness, I prayed and found comfort and direction from David's example in the Psalms. David often cried out to God with his fears, doubts, faith – and praise.

The two years during which Steven was being treated for cancer were an emotionally desperate time. But through it all, I kept talking to God. When Steven passed away, I had to keep praying. God was refining my faith. Over time, I was able to see the many ways God had loved Steven and cared for me.

Life can change suddenly for any of us through illness, loss of a job, the end of a relationship or some other disaster. In these and every event in our lives, we can find strength and comfort through prayer and reading God's word.

Prayer: *Faithful God, when we are overwhelmed, help us turn to you for help – the way David did. Amen*

Thought for the day: God is my refuge and source of help.

Carol Van Der Woude (Illinois, US)

First Sunday in Lent

Read Matthew 13:1–8

Other seeds fell on good soil and brought forth grain, some a hundredfold, some sixty, some thirty. Let anyone with ears listen!
Matthew 13:8–9 (NRSV)

When my children were young, our family had fun playing with sparklers – those wand-like fireworks that emit colourful sparks and flashes. They enjoyed watching the sparklers swirl in the air, leaving fleeting traces of whirls and swooshes in the darkness. For all their bling and pizzazz, though, sparklers don't last very long. Little twinges of disappointment would show on my children's faces each time a sparkler ran its course and fizzled out.

Sometimes the excitement that comes from becoming a Christian – or even an energising spiritual experience – can seem much like a sparkler. It's grand, showy and feels great, but if it is grounded only in a surge of emotion then the excitement is likely to fizzle out.

The authentic Christian experience is less like a sparkler and more akin to a warming fire. It takes effort to get it started and discipline and persistence to keep it fed and glowing. But it will never go out as long as we are willing to do the work of nurturing it. On our daily walk with Christ, we stoke that fire with Bible study, prayer, meditation and through sharing God's love with others. Working to keep that fire burning within us through good times and bad gives us a warm sense of God's presence.

Prayer: *Dear God, help us to kindle the flame of faith so that we remain committed to you. Amen*

Thought for the day: I will begin – and end – this day walking with Christ.

David McCain (Louisiana, US)

Something better

Read Philippians 3:1–14

Store up for yourselves treasures in heaven, where neither moth nor rust consumes and where thieves do not break in and steal.
Matthew 6:20 (NRSV)

When our children were young, their curious minds often attracted them to things they should not have been touching. My natural response tended toward what I called a 'King Kong' approach: seizing the item out of their fingers or mouth and giving them a fearsome look so they would be afraid to pick up that item in the future. My wife usually had a much different approach. She offered our children something safer and more attractive to play with. They chose to let go of the first item to take the new offering.

Jesus uses much the same approach with us. It is easy to base our lives on our own wants and desires. But Jesus offers us the riches of his kingdom and life eternal if we will only release our tight grip on the things we've collected. Jesus gives us the gift of faith to help us, so that we might realise that his kingdom is far more real and infinitely more valuable than anything we could desire on earth.

Prayer: *Dear Lord, open our eyes to see the riches you've stored for us. Amen*

Thought for the day: How can I follow my faith instead of my worldly desires?

Charles Huff (Illinois, US)

Do not worry

Read Matthew 6:25–34

[The Lord said to all the Israelites], 'During the forty years that I led you through the wilderness, your clothes did not wear out, nor did the sandals on your feet.'
Deuteronomy 29:5 (NIV)

Eight years ago when I faced the decision of whether to leave a good job in order to care for my children full time, God spoke to me through today's quoted verse. God cared for the people of Israel in a very practical way – their sandals did not wear out! This helped me to believe that God cares about the details of our lives and provides for them. It gave me the courage to leave work and have faith that he would look after our family. It was not always easy, but God looked after us month by month, year by year.

Recently our circumstances changed, and I began to worry. Is it time for me to go back to work? How can I find a job that will allow me to earn yet still be able to care for our boys? We prayed, and God answered in a wonderfully practical way. Someone at church – who was unaware of our situation – approached me and asked if I would be interested in a job where she worked. I could hardly believe it when I found out that the job was exactly what I needed in terms of working hours and flexibility. I accepted the job with a heart full of gratitude. We are meeting all of our family's needs, and I have learned once again to trust our God who leads us and cares for us.

Prayer: *Thank you, Lord, for being our great provider. Help us to trust that you will care for us all our lives. Amen*

Thought for the day: God cares about the details of my life.

Julie Ann Brown (Antrim, Northern Ireland)

God's patio

Read Philippians 4:4–9

You who answer prayer, to you all people will come.
Psalm 65:2 (NIV)

While I was visiting my friend in South Carolina, we loved to sink into the wicker chairs on her patio, sip our morning coffee and chat about anything and everything. Some topics brought laughter and others brought tears. We knew each other well enough to share our deepest thoughts without fear of judgement or ridicule. Our words flowed easily as we talked about memories, hopes and current struggles. Every morning I looked forward to this precious time with my friend.

That made me think about my prayer time with God. I used to struggle with prayer until one day I began to see it as a time to sit on God's 'patio' and chat awhile. God welcomes me to come any time and stay as long as I want. He never sends me away empty but instead fills my cup and feeds me the bread of life that my soul hungers for. As we sit and chat, I learn more about him and about myself. Through these prayer times I have learned that he is my trusted friend with whom I can talk about anything.

Spending time with him gives me a clearer picture of things, and I gain strength. I may have climbed those steps to God's 'patio' with a heavy heart, but after we have talked I am refreshed. I finish my day with a much lighter spirit because I have taken the time to be with God, my friend.

Prayer: *Dear God, help us to take the time to sit and listen when we pray so that we may come to know you better. Amen*

Thought for the day: Spending time with God refreshes my soul.

Linda Fasking (Kentucky, US)

Lord of time

Read Ephesians 5:15–16

Be careful then how you live, not as unwise people but as wise, making the most of the time, because the days are evil.
Ephesians 5:15 (NRSV)

When we enter a new year, we cannot ignore the passing of time. We may feel that time passes more quickly than it used to, but we know that there are the same number of hours in a day and days in a week as in the past year. Though we may regret the passing of time, we cannot turn the clock back.

We don't have the choice of that celebrated TV Time Lord, Dr Who. We cannot reinvent ourselves innumerable times, as Dr Who succeeds in doing. I wonder if the programme's fascination lies in the doctor's ability to defeat time.

We may like to go back to our younger selves, but we cannot go back and change the past, even for a fraction of a second. Nor can we retract one angry word or selfish act. But we do have a choice about the future. We have a God who is Lord of all time, past, present and future, and he can be Lord of our time too. We can place our present and future in his hands, to live the life he wants us to live.

Though we don't have the fantastical powers of TV science fiction characters, we have a greater power in God, who promises to be with us this year and in all our years to come.

Prayer: *Dear God, we thank you that every second, minute and day of our lives is in your hands. Amen*

Thought for the day: Time passes and the years roll by, but God is always the same.

Anne Rasmussen (Somerset, UK)

The family of God

Read 1 Corinthians 12:12–20
We were all baptised by one Spirit so as to form one body.
1 Corinthians 12:13 (NIV)

For our wedding anniversary, my husband and I received a picture designed with letter tiles from a Scrabble game. The letters created a crossword puzzle with my name, my husband's name, and the names of all our children and grandchildren – depicting a family interdependent and united. Each letter was secured in place with glue. If even one letter were removed, the entire effect would be destroyed.

Because the puzzle is displayed prominently on our living room wall, we look at it often. The image of our interconnecting names helps us to feel closer to the members of our family who live at a distance. No, we do not always live in perfect harmony. No family does.

Church families do not always live in perfect harmony either. In writing to the church at Corinth, Paul used the human body as a metaphor for how the church family should work. Paul's words remind us that we each have an important role to play in the work of God's kingdom. Just as each letter in our crossword puzzle was vital to the whole picture, each person in the church is as important as the next in God's kingdom. The question we each must ask ourselves is this: am I where God wants me to be, doing what he wants me to be doing, today?

Prayer: *Thy kingdom come, O God, thy will be done – on earth as it is in heaven. Amen*

Thought for the day: I have an important role in God's kingdom.

Madeline Peterson (Nebraska, US)

Christmas all year

Read Matthew 1:18–25

They will call him, Emmanuel. (Emmanuel means 'God with us.')
Matthew 1:23 (CEB)

One Christmas we received a clock that chimes the tune of a Christmas hymn every hour on the hour. We enjoyed listening to the clock throughout Advent and Christmas. In the new year, I took down the clock and was ready to store it until the following Christmas season when my husband asked me not to pack it away. He thoroughly enjoyed listening to the chimes since they reminded him of the meaning of Christmas.

At first I thought it odd listening to Christmas melodies in March and June and September. But the reason to celebrate Christmas – the coming of God in the flesh – is the foundation of our faith and our reason to live every single day of the year. Throughout the year we do not know what situations we will encounter. Some will be agreeable; others will not. But the gospel message in Matthew of the birth of the child Jesus reassures us: 'Emmanuel'. God is always with us, throughout the year.

Prayer: *God of infinite goodness, thank you for walking with us every day of the year. Amen*

Thought for the day: The birth of Jesus promises that God is with me every day.

Priscila Laguna Y Acuña (Puebla, México)

PRAYER FOCUS: TO REMEMBER THE GIFT OF JESUS ALL YEAR

Second Sunday in Lent

Read Psalm 126:1–6

The Lord has done great things for us, and we are filled with joy.
Psalm 126:3 (NIV)

At times the mundane parts of life can make me lose my sense of joy in the Lord. I know that writing a paper for college or doing everyday tasks does not make me jump up and shout, 'Hallelujah!' But I am learning during these moments to turn my attention to Christ and all that he has done for me. And this fills me with gratitude and gives me a better perspective.

Even psychologists emphasise that a disposition of gratitude promotes healthy living and joy. The Bible – especially the book of Psalms – is full of gratitude and praise for all God's good works. Paul expresses thankfulness in all of his letters. Of course, the greatest act to be thankful for is Christ's sacrifice on the cross. Even a glimpse of what the suffering, death and resurrection of Christ accomplished for us will fill us with joy unspeakable.

Prayer: *Dear Father, we give thanks for all you have done. Restore to us the joy of your salvation (see Psalm 51:12). As Jesus taught us, we pray, 'Our Father which art in heaven, Hallowed be thy name. Thy kingdom come. Thy will be done, as in heaven, so in earth. Give us day by day our daily bread. And forgive us our sins; for we also forgive every one that is indebted to us. And lead us not into temptation; but deliver us from evil.'* Amen*

Thought for the day: Today I will think of all God has done for me and let my gratitude inspire joy!

Hindrek Taavet Taimla (Võru, Estonia)

Belief and doubt

Read Mark 9:14–29

The father of the child cried out, 'I believe; help my unbelief!'
Mark 9:24 (NRSV)

My daughter has been ill for over two years. We've seen numerous doctors and specialists but have received few answers. Time after time, doctors have said they can't help her. This situation makes it easy for me to relate to the father in Mark 9. Feeling worn down and helpless, he believes but still questions whether healing is even possible. I believe in miracles; but when disappointment and discouragement start to overwhelm me, doubts grow and I wonder if change is possible.

How can I believe and doubt at the same time? When we are struggling with chronic illness or grief or family crises, all we can see is where we are at the moment. Some days it's hard to keep believing that things will change. But like the father in today's reading, we can confess our doubts and ask God to help our unbelief. This gives us strength to keep going and reminds us that with God, all things are possible – even healing and the relief of pain after years of illness.

Prayer: *Dear God, thank you for allowing us to confess our doubts and unbelief to you. Help us in our unbelief. In Jesus' name we pray. Amen*

Thought for the day: God listens when I confess my doubts and gives me strength to keep going.

Laura Rath (Iowa, US)

A grateful heart

Read Exodus 16:1–15

Lord, you alone are my portion and my cup; you make my lot secure.
Psalm 16:5 (NIV)

My friend worked night shifts, but because of many health and family issues, he really needed a daytime job. When I told my friend to pray for help in finding another job, he said, 'I don't want to be a bother to God.' My friend thought that his need was unimportant to God. Thankfully, God doesn't view us and our needs as inconveniences! He wants a relationship with each of us and is eager to hear from us about our concerns and problems.

In today's reading about the Israelites complaining and worrying about what they were going to eat, I noticed that God provided for them even though their attitudes were ungrateful. So if we go to God with a grateful attitude, how much more will he pour blessings upon us?

God cares about all of our challenges – even the seemingly trivial ones. Our Creator wants to be involved in every part of our lives. When we remember that God is bigger than our worries and concerns, we can approach him with a thankful heart.

Prayer: *Dear God, help me to bring all of my concerns to you – no matter how small. In Jesus' name I pray. Amen*

Thought for the day: Today I will turn to God with even my smallest needs.

Tammy Teeter (Tennessee, US)

PRAYER FOCUS: SOMEONE SEARCHING FOR A JOB

Childlike faith

Read Matthew 18:1–3

Unless you change and become like little children, you will never enter the kingdom of heaven.
Matthew 18:3 (NIV)

Although I was brought up to go to church, I became an atheist as a teenager and did not regain faith in God until near the end of my university studies. However, while I came to believe that God existed and that Christianity was true, my scepticism did not disappear. If anything, as a Christian, I questioned even more.

This made for some awkward moments in church. Whereas many of my friends could simply accept things in faith, I would ask questions that made people feel uncomfortable. 'Why can't you just have childlike faith?' they would ask. This caused me to wonder if I was a bad Christian because I asked too many questions or because having faith does not always come easily.

The answer came when I became a father. My children are very curious and inquisitive. They want to know why things are the way they are and simple answers will not do. The more answers I give them, the more questions they have for me. I realised that childlike faith has nothing to do with refusing to ask questions. In truth, no one asks more questions than a child.

We are called to a childlike faith – a faith that has room for questions. We can trust God's goodness even as we wrestle with the mysteries of life.

Prayer: *Dear God, thank you for hearing our questions. Help us to trust in you more and more each day. Amen*

Thought for the day: God embraces my questions.

Stephen J. Bedard (Ontario, Canada)

To bless and be blessed

One of my common closings for letters or emails has been, 'Blessings'. To me this seemed like a way to express my prayerful goodwill toward the recipient. When we say to someone, 'May God bless you', I think we often mean, 'I pray God will care for you, protect you, or comfort you.' But I listened to a sermon recently and realised that the blessings mentioned in scripture are far more complex than simple goodwill or favour, and that God's blessing often bestows responsibility as well. I began to wonder what it means to bless and to be blessed, so I went looking for answers in scripture.

Two different Greek words are often translated 'blessed' in English versions of scripture. The verb *eulogeo* means 'to ask for God's special favour'. We use this meaning of 'blessing' when we pray before a meal, and this is the meaning I intend when I sign my letters, 'Blessings'. The second word for blessing, *makarios*, caught my attention. *Makarios* is the word translated as 'blessed' or 'happy' in Matthew 5, the passage known as the Beatitudes. Jesus says to his disciples, 'Blessed are the poor in spirit... those who mourn... those who are persecuted for righteousness' sake...' (Matthew 5:3–4, 10, NRSV). To be *makarios*, 'blessed', is not something we possess or something that's bestowed upon us; it's something we embody, something we are.

If *eulogeo* asks for God's favour, *makarios* tells us what our lives look like when we are favoured by God. This kind of blessing is about what is important to God and how he views the world. In the New Testament, Jesus uses *makarios* to describe masters who wash the feet of their servants, hosts who serve guests who cannot repay them, those who do not take offence at the blind gaining sight, the dead being raised to life and good news being given to the poor.

Peter, who perceives God's truth and names Jesus as the Messiah, is *makarios*. Mary, who believes God's message that her son will save the world, is *makarios*. This kind of blessing is not superficial or fleeting happiness. It is not the absence of pain or sorrow. Instead, it is the happiness that comes from the hope of finding comfort in mourning, of receiving mercy and of knowing God. Isn't this the kind of blessing we all long for? Truly to know God and share in what makes him happy? *Makarios* is surely more lasting and fulfilling than any material gift or bounty.

This lasting blessing is not just about you or me as individuals, though. Jesus uses the plural form of the word. A better translation of the Beatitudes might be: you all will have the joy of knowing God's happiness when you are poor in spirit, for the kingdom of heaven belongs to all of you. You all will have the joy of knowing God's happiness when you mourn, for all of you will be comforted. The Beatitudes remind us that no matter what trial or sorrow we experience we are not alone. 'Blessed are all of you who mourn, for you will be comforted.' *Makarios* brings us together in our suffering and challenges us to act for the good of others – to comfort those who mourn, to give and receive mercy, to be peacemakers. When we do, you and I and all of God's beloved community can have the joy of knowing God more deeply. May we all be so blessed.

Several meditations in this issue deal with themes of blessing and community engagement. Consider reading the following meditations again as you reflect: January 2, 6, 7, 10, 12, 21; February 2, 27; March 2 and 29; and April 7, 10 and 25.

Questions for reflection

1 When you think of being blessed by God, what comes to mind? Are blessings material or spiritual for you?

2 What would it look like for your community to be blessed in the *makarios* way? How would people behave differently? What can you do to help create this kind of blessed community?

Lindsay Gray
Editorial Director, The Upper Room

Filling bigger shoes

Read Exodus 4:10–17

Trust in the Lord with all your heart and lean not on your own under-standing; in all your ways submit to him, and he will make your paths straight.

Proverbs 3:5–6 (NIV)

One Sunday during the sermon, our minister illustrated how hard it is to walk in someone else's shoes. We all had a good laugh as the pastor tried to walk in children's shoes and the children in the congregation tried to wear adult-sized shoes.

As I listened, it occurred to me that I often struggle to 'fill the shoes' the Lord is asking me to wear. Sometimes I do not feel capable or qualified to take on a new task or responsibility. But then I recall God's response to Moses in today's reading, when Moses complained that he was slow of speech and did not want to be a leader. I take comfort, trusting that if I am willing to follow God's call, then he will help me to fill those shoes.

At other times I hesitate because I don't want to give up something I enjoy doing in order to serve God. But then I reflect on the sacrifice Jesus made for us, and I'm humbled. I know that regardless of my shortcomings, the Lord is always there, ready and waiting for me to follow.

Prayer: *Heavenly Father, thank you for reminding us that we can serve you in new and unique ways. Open our eyes and hearts to serve you better each day. Amen*

Thought for the day: What shoes will God call me to fill today?

Randy Bury (Tennessee, US)

Consider it a gift

Read Matthew 10:1–8

We have received, not the spirit of the world, but the spirit which is of God; that we might know the things that are freely given to us of God.
1 Corinthians 2:12 (KJV)

When I discovered I would be late for lunch with a friend, I sent a text message asking her to order my meal for me. We enjoyed a long chat over good food. On my way home I realised that my friend had not only ordered my food for me, but she had also paid for it. I called her with an apology and a promise to repay her. 'Consider it a gift,' she said.

'You are very kind,' I said, 'but please let me buy your lunch the next time we meet.'

'I wanted to bless you with my gift,' she said. 'Please allow me to enjoy the blessing of giving with no expectation of receiving.' This was hard for me to do. However, I realised that giving without expecting anything in return is God's way of giving.

Every day we receive many gifts from God. We have not earned these gifts and cannot possibly repay them. He generously gives good gifts. We can graciously accept gifts given to us, whether given by God or by other people. When we receive gifts given in kindness without expectation of repayment, we allow others to experience the blessing they can receive by giving as God gives.

Prayer: *Dear Lord, help us be generous givers and grateful receivers, so that in all things you may receive the glory. Amen*

Thought for the day: What gift is God inviting me to receive graciously today?

Debra Scales (Indiana, US)

True worth

Read 1 Samuel 16:1–13

'Who can hide in secret places so that I cannot see them?' declares the Lord. 'Do not I fill heaven and earth?' declares the Lord.
Jeremiah 23:24 (NIV)

Some time ago, I went to buy a used car. I was tempted merely to look at the outward appearance and then check the price tag on the front window. Luckily I remembered my father's comment that it is easy to polish a car on the surface but harder to treat the rust underneath. Sure enough! When I looked at the underside of the cars, I discovered that several of the cars I was considering looked perfect from the outside but were actually corroded with rust underneath. It would have been unwise to buy any one of them.

In a similar way, God can see the true nature of human beings. Nothing can be kept secret from God (see Jeremiah 23:24). Nor is there anything that won't be revealed eventually (see Luke 12:2). David was a man after God's own heart (1 Samuel 13:14), chosen and valued for his character. When we are tempted to judge others, we need first to measure ourselves by the godliness of our behaviour.

Prayer: *O God, thank you for knowing us completely. Help us to live so that others may see you in us. As Jesus taught us, we pray, 'Father, hallowed be your name, your kingdom come. Give us each day our daily bread. Forgive us our sins, for we also forgive everyone who sins against us. And lead us not into temptation.'* Amen

Thought for the day: I will value myself and others by looking at the heart the way God does.

Hindrek Taavet Taimla (Estonia)

Third Sunday in Lent

Read Ephesians 4:17–31

Do not conform to the pattern of this world, but be transformed by the renewing of your mind. Then you will be able to test and approve what God's will is – his good, pleasing and perfect will.
Romans 12:2 (NIV)

I look forward to my annual spring cleaning. I enjoy opening the windows while I clean deep into the forgotten corners of my home. I rummage through drawers and cupboards eliminating all old, worn and unnecessary items. It's hard work, and I'm always amazed at how much useless stuff I manage to accumulate.

I'm grateful for the opportunity to clean up, throw out and prepare for a new season. I am equally grateful for the season of Lent and the opportunity to employ a similar process in my spiritual life. I rummage through and deep clean the forgotten corners of my mind and spirit to find what useless stuff I've allowed to accumulate there. Often, I find that I hold on to jealousy, hurt feelings or resentment. Through focused attention and prayer, I am able to use this season to purge spiritual clutter from my life.

Jesus Christ spent the period before his crucifixion in prayer and meditation preparing for his resurrection. We can prepare for the commemoration of our Lord's resurrection in the same way. Through this practice we can experience renewal.

Prayer: *Gracious Lord, give us the wisdom to recognise what needs to be eliminated from our lives, and the strength to follow through. Amen*

Thought for the day: Lent offers me the chance to refresh and renew my faith.

Monica A. Andermann (New York, US)

A career in ministry

Read Mark 1:9–20

[Jesus] said to them, 'Go into all the world and preach the gospel to all creation.'
Mark 16:15 (NIV)

When I was at high school, I wanted to work in a church. I also achieved good exam results. For one of my classmates who wasn't a believer, those two things – working in a church and being clever – didn't go together. I still remember a conversation we had sitting in our school's gym. 'You're clever. You could do anything. Why would you want to waste all that on a church?'

That conversation was a long time ago, but I still reflect on it often. I did work for a church for a time, but most of my career has been with other organisations. Do I feel that I've wasted my potential? Of course not. I've come to realise that I could have had any career and still been in ministry.

Jesus calls us to 'Go into all the world and preach.' Ministry isn't limited to the church; it also happens in our communities. People in all types of careers work for God every day – doctors, bus drivers, restaurant waiters, plumbers, teachers; the list goes on. Wherever we are, we can all minister by being open and sharing God's love with others.

Prayer: *Dear Lord, help us to recognise ways to be a witness for you each and every day. Amen*

Thought for the day: How can I minister to the people in my life today?

Catherine Ryan (South Carolina, US)

Lost and found

Read Matthew 18:10–14

Jesus said, 'The Son of Man came to seek out and to save the lost.'
Luke 19:10 (NRSV)

A favourite game we played as children was hide-and-seek with Copper, our golden retriever. We would take turns holding Copper while the rest of us hid in the deep woods. Once released, a determined Copper would relentlessly search until he found everyone. He would gently take each of us by the sleeve or cuff and bring us safely home – every time!

This game helps me relate to the parable of the lost sheep, one of Jesus' most compelling parables. It speaks volumes about his passion for his disciples and reveals the extravagant love of God.

Knowing Jesus would go after just one of his lost sheep – even me – fills my heart with assurance and joy. My own journey with Jesus has been filled with times of getting lost. Sometimes it's because of failure, pain, impatience or seeking the pleasures of the world. But in such times of wandering, I have learned that we need not hide from Jesus in fear or regret, because our Good Shepherd is the one who will never let us go. When we cry out to him, Jesus will find us and carry us back home!

Prayer: *O God, thank you for never giving up on us. In the name of our Good Shepherd. Amen*

Thought for the day: The greatest feeling in the world is to be found by God's love.

James Baumberger (Connecticut, US)

Not-so-quiet time with God

Read Psalm 150:1–6

Let everything that breathes praise the Lord!
Psalm 150:6 (NRSV)

For many people, being alone with God means 'quiet time' without interference from the outside world. However, because I am an extrovert, quietness is not in my nature.

When I pray, I have found it easier to speak aloud to God as though speaking to a human friend. My quiet time can also include singing. Sometimes I sing the words of a hymn or a praise song which connect with the biblical words I have been studying. Occasionally my time alone with God is accompanied by the sound of weeping – tears shed for a family tragedy or for the state of the world. Finally there are times I need to shout out loud in anger or frustration toward God. But more often my shouts have been those of joy and happiness that mere words cannot express.

The psalmist knew something about a quiet time that isn't so quiet. Psalm 147:1 says, 'How good it is to sing praises to our God.' Psalm 150 invites the trumpet, harp, tambourine, lute, cymbals and strings to join with everything that has breath to praise the Lord!

Prayer: *Whether silent or spoken, whether noisy or quiet, may our praise and thanksgiving be pleasing to you, O God. Amen*

Thought for the day: Time with God does not have to be quiet.

Carol Purves (Cumbria, England)

Holding hands

Read John 14:1–12

Jesus said, 'The one who believes in me will also do the works that I do.'
John 14:12 (NRSV)

Recently a number of people have commented about my wife and me holding hands. One friend remarked, 'Well, look at you two!' Once while we were strolling in our neighbourhood, a woman walking her dog stopped to tell us how sweet we looked. My wife summed it up later when she asked, 'Is it because we are in our sixties that holding hands has now become sweet to see?'

We hope that this small show of affection sends a message that most people can understand. Besides saying that we still love each other after 43 years, our holding hands also says that we are a team. We belong with each other.

When I think of my relationship with Jesus, I wonder if people see that I love him and belong to him. Do the ways I respond to hurtful people and experiences declare my love for Jesus?

We show that we belong to Jesus when we reflect that we are one with him in the way we respond in every situation. When we act the way Jesus would, others can see that we belong to him. As we walk through life with Jesus, nothing can separate us from his love (see Romans 8:38–39).

Prayer: *Dear Jesus, help us to draw close to you so that we can reflect more of your love to others. Amen*

Thought for the day: Today I will reflect the love of Jesus by what I say and do.

Charles Huff (Illinois, US)

Don't give up

Read Psalm 121:1–6

I lift up my eyes to the mountains – where does my help come from? My help comes from the Lord, the Maker of heaven and earth.
Psalm 121:1–2 (NIV)

Because my husband works in another city, I have the responsibility of taking care of our two teenage sons and my elderly mother-in-law. Sometimes my life gets stressful as I try to manage everything alone.

Recently, I was driving my family to worship on Sunday morning. I wanted to reach the church at least 20 minutes before the service began because I was helping to lead the worship. Halfway through our journey, the car had a flat tyre. There was hardly any time to replace it, so my only option was to park the car and to try to contact another church member to say that I would not make it to the service on time.

As I stood there with my family, a car stopped near us. What a surprise! It was a member of our church driving by. She was alone so we could all fit in her car. As I helped to lead the worship that morning, I was overwhelmed with gratitude to God for being mindful of our needs.

When difficult situations leave us desperate and ready to give up, God is still working! He knows our needs and will surely respond to our prayers for help.

Prayer: *Dear heavenly Father, thank you for your unending love. In times of distress and weakness, strengthen and renew us. In Jesus' name we pray. Amen*

Thought for the day: God always surprises me.

Sahana Mathias (Bangalore, India)

PRAYER FOCUS: SINGLE PARENTS

The way of the cross

Read Mark 15:16–24

Show me your ways, Lord, teach me your paths. Guide me in your truth and teach me, for you are God my Saviour, and my hope is in you all day long.
Psalm 25:4–5 (NIV)

A rutted, red-dirt road wound its way to the summit of the hill, on which stood a cross. All the way up stood marble 'Stations of the Cross', and as I sat by one of them, I had a vision of Jesus, battered and blood-ied, bowed under the weight of his cross, struggling up a hill like this. I heard the jeers of the crowd and witnessed the look of sorrow and pain as he staggered to the place of his execution, not on the island of Gozo, where I was, but on the hill of Calvary.

Then I saw the cross, and Jesus' lifeblood flowing down to wash me clean from all my sins and shortcomings. I turned, and saw the rest of my life, like a golden road running down the hill and snaking out over the dark moor of the world. I knew that, by accepting Christ's sacrifice on a daily basis, he would light up the road as I walk it in companion-ship with him.

Prayer: *Lord, teach me your ways, and never let go of my hand on the road of my life. Amen*

Thought for the day: Today I will stand at the foot of the cross and remember the sacrifice Jesus made.

Carol B. Logan (Berkshire, England)

Fourth Sunday in Lent

Read Psalm 46:1–11

Be still, and know that I am God.
Psalm 46:10 (NIV)

Within a period of ten months, eleven family members, friends and a work colleague had died. My 14-year-old cousin had been killed while crossing the road at night. And my 23-year-old niece, who had just won her battle with leukaemia, died from an unrelated cause. My heart ached as I tried to reach out to the parents of those who had died while also dealing with my own grief.

How can I find peace in the midst of loss and troubling times? This question ran through my mind often as I searched the scriptures for solace. Over and over I was drawn to Psalm 46:10. As I continued to read this psalm, I realised that my hope is not in this world but in God and his promises. Time and again, I'm encouraged to let God be my refuge and strength, a helper in my times of trouble.

As Jesus was getting ready to leave his disciples, he told them to take courage because he was going to prepare a place for them and was also leaving them his peace. His was a peace that is not found in this world. As we go to God with thanksgivings and petitions, we have his promise of a peace that passes all our understanding (see Philippians 4:7). God's peace is a deep, abiding peace in times of trouble and grief.

Prayer: *Father God, thank you for being our place of refuge and our strength when life is difficult. In Jesus' name. Amen*

Thought for the day: God is my source of peace in troubling times.

Jodi C. Czabajszki (Texas, US)

Welcome the stranger

Read Matthew 25:31–40

The King will say to those on his right... 'I was hungry and you gave me something to eat, I was thirsty and you gave me something to drink, I was a stranger and you invited me in.'

Matthew 25:34–35 (NIV)

During World War II many people in the US lacked the basics of life – food and shelter – just as many do today. On a particular rainy winter's day in South Louisiana in 1944, I spotted a man crossing our neighbour's garden. He was dishevelled, and he approached our back door holding something in his hands. I ran to tell my grandmother, who was in the kitchen cooking. As she opened the door, we saw that he was holding a large piece of meat. He looked up at us with an expression of desperation I'll never forget and said, 'Lady, would you cook this meat for me?'

My grandmother said, 'Come in out of the cold, and I will do that for you.' As I watched, she prepared the meat, added other food from the family dinner she was cooking, and served the stranger at our kitchen table. While he hungrily ate the hot food, we hung his wet coat in front of our little gas fire to dry. Soon he was on his way. If we are alert to the needs of others, each of us can prepare to respond to the stranger at the door as if that stranger were Jesus.

Prayer: *Dear God, give us the compassion to open our eyes, our hearts and our doors to others. Amen*

Thought for the day: The next time I see someone in need, I will serve Christ by offering help.

Charles E. Shea (Texas, US)

Unexpected generosity

Read Psalm 139:1–6

The Lord does not look at the things people look at. People look at the outward appearance, but the Lord looks at the heart.
1 Samuel 16:7 (NIV)

One Sunday afternoon as my husband and I waited in the church foyer for a meeting to start, a man who knew about the church's ministry with those experiencing homelessness came in to ask us for bus money. We gave him some money and he went on his way. A few minutes later a second man appeared. We expected another request for money. Instead, to our surprise, he held out a sum of money and said that he wanted to make a donation to our church. In that instant, our stereotyped views of people who experience homelessness were turned upside down. We were amazed at the generosity of this man who seemed to have so little.

In 1 Samuel 16, the prophet Samuel was sent to anoint one of Jesse's sons as king. As each of Jesse's seven oldest sons stood before Samuel, the prophet was certain that each one would be the one chosen. However, God reminded Samuel in today's verse that God looks at the heart, not the outward appearance. Finally, the youngest son, David, was anointed with God's blessing.

That donation reminded me to look beyond appearance to what a person's actions reveal about their heart. No matter what our appearance or our faults are, God loves us and shows us how to love one another.

Prayer: *Thank you, Lord, that you know us through and through, yet still love us. Help us to accept others and to see them as you do. Amen*

Thought for the day: God loves me, faults and all.

Margaret Anne Martin (Capital Territory, Australia)

Lighten the load

Read Matthew 11:28–30

Cast all your anxiety on [God], because he cares for you.
1 Peter 5:7 (NRSV)

Several years ago, I decided to start living in a healthier way. After eating better and exercising I lost three and a half stone. I slept better, my knees and feet stopped hurting, and my cholesterol dropped. But I didn't know how big a difference I'd made until I went on a walking holiday. We hiked 18 miles in three days with all our supplies on our backs. My pack weighed 50 pounds. As I walked along the paths, I was amazed that I had carried that same amount of weight every day for years.

Just as I was carrying too much physical weight, many of us are weighed down by guilt and shame. Broken relationships leave us clinging to grudges. The weight of our struggles piles on so gradually that we often don't realise how it is affecting us. We are not designed for this weight! The season of Lent grants us the opportunity to lighten our loads. As we take a closer look at ourselves during these 40 days, we can find weights to lay down. Today's verse reminds us that giving our worries to God can heal us. Through prayer, we can let go of what holds us back and find the freedom that comes in Jesus.

Prayer: *Dear Jesus, help us surrender our burdens to you so that we may live joyfully. Amen*

Thought for the day: What Lenten practice will help me to live more freely in Christ?

Kevin L. Thomas (Alabama, US)

Streams of living water

Read Psalm 1:1–6

Those who trust in the Lord... shall be like a tree planted by water, sending out its roots by the stream. It shall not fear when heat comes, and its leaves shall stay green; in the year of drought it is not anxious.
Jeremiah 17:7–8 (NRSV)

Before I was born, my grandfather bought a lake cabin on a winding country road. I love walking there; the road is paved now, but it still feels secluded – close to nature and to God. The road follows a clear stream that bubbles up from underground. Even on a hot July day, this area is refreshingly shady and cool because of the huge trees that line the banks of the stream. These majestic trees are old and unusually large due to the steady supply of water. Their roots reach toward the stream like outstretched hands.

When I read the verses above, I picture those trees, tall and green, lining the bank. The verses remind me that spiritual growth results from a consistent supply of living water from God's word and presence. Jesus said, 'Whoever drinks the water I give them will never thirst' (John 4:14).

Spending time with the Lord refreshes our souls. When we reach out to God – through Bible study and prayer – we receive that living water. Immersing ourselves in God's word each day brings us a vibrant spiritual life and keeps our lives joyful and strong, even in times of drought.

Prayer: *Dear Lord, refresh us with streams of living water so that we may grow strong and bear fruit, even during our struggles. In Jesus' name. Amen*

Thought for the day: Today I can be refreshed by living water as I spend time with God.

May Patterson (Alabama, US)

Looking or seeing?

Read 2 Timothy 3:14–17

Open my eyes that I may see wonderful things in your law... do not hide your commands from me.
Psalm 119:18–19 (NIV)

Trying to remember where I'd put my keys, I ran from room to room. Surely, they had to be nearby! I checked coat pockets, the kitchen table and the small desk near the phone. I didn't want to waste more time, but I needed those keys! My teenage daughter's question stopped me in my tracks. 'Mum, have you prayed about finding the keys?' I had not. I sat down on the stairs, bowed my head, and asked God to help me. As I opened my eyes and raised my head, I looked straight at the keys. They were hanging beside the door. In my search, I had walked past that door many times, missing what was in plain sight.

Sometimes we read the Bible and it just doesn't make sense to us. Jesus appeared to the disciples after his resurrection and reminded them of what he had told them earlier and 'opened their minds so they could understand the Scriptures' (Luke 24:45, NIV). If the ones who travelled with Jesus needed his help to understand scripture, it's not surprising that we would need to seek this help through prayer. Every time we pause to spend time reading scripture, we can pray that the Holy Spirit will open our eyes and guide us to new insights.

Prayer: *Dear heavenly Father, help us to take the time to listen for your guidance so that we may understand what we read in the Bible. Amen*

Thought for the day: I will pray to understand God's word more fully.

Pat Gerbrandt (Manitoba, Canada)

On a desert island

Read Romans 5:1–8

Hope does not put us to shame, because God's love has been poured out into our hearts through the Holy Spirit, who has been given to us.
Romans 5:5 (NIV)

I speak at leadership conferences for businesses and organisations. I like to start my sessions by asking the group a question to spark conversation: if you were going to be left on a desert island all by yourself, what one item would you choose to take with you and why?

I love the responses to this question. The things I have heard and the reasons behind them are always fascinating to me: a microwave, a photo of family, a comb, a Bible, matches, underwear, a pen – the list goes on. It is not about the item itself as much as it is about the hope that the item brings to each person. Although some of the items seem silly and useless on a desert island, each has the ability to help a person hold on to the courage to continue looking forward.

While some comfort can be found in objects, our ultimate hope is in Jesus Christ, who gives us hope to endure all our difficult circumstances – divorce, sickness, unemployment or whatever our personal desert island might be. Today's quoted verse assures us that we can find comfort when we keep our focus on Jesus Christ.

Prayer: *Dear Jesus, you are our hope in every circumstance. Even when we feel stranded, we know we can trust in you. Amen*

Thought for the day: Jesus gives me strength to endure all my trials.

Todd Diedrich (Wisconsin, US)

Fifth Sunday in Lent

Read Mark 15:22–32

God so loved the world that he gave his one and only Son, that whoever believes in him shall not perish but have eternal life.
John 3:16 (NIV)

When I was young, I would go to a small town in Pennsylvania to visit my mother's grandmother. My great-grandmother encouraged me to walk into town. I was frightened that I would not be able to find my way back, but she told me that if I would just stand in front of the main shop's big window and look up the hill I would be able to see her house and that she would be there. After that I never feared becoming lost.

Years later, I returned to her small town. My great-grandmother was long gone, but we stopped in front of the store so I could look up the hill and recall the kind, wonderful woman and the love that had waited for me there.

We are in the season of Lent. During this journey, we start to look toward another hill, one known as Golgotha. We will once again remember the Last Supper, the trial and the crucifixion. But then Easter Sunday will come. When I am lost, confused or frightened, I look toward that hill and know that I can find salvation there. Christ loves us so much that he suffered and laid down his life on that hill. Just as my great-grandmother always waited for me on her hill in Pennsylvania, Christ is waiting, ready to welcome all of us.

Prayer: *Dear Lord, remind us to look toward that hill where we find our salvation. Help us to reach out to others with your love and to lead them to you. In the name of Jesus Christ. Amen*

Thought for the day: Christ waits for me with great love.

Grace A. Epperson (Michigan, US)

Speak no evil

Read James 3:3–12

The words of the reckless pierce like swords, but the tongue of the wise brings healing.
Proverbs 12:18 (NIV)

I know that gossiping and speaking ill of others is a sin, yet I still fall into this behaviour constantly – and even blame others for my failure. If that colleague were not so annoying, I would not complain about her to others. If only my neighbour would bring her dog in when he was barking, I wouldn't talk to the other neighbours about her inconsiderate behaviour. The truth is, I make the choice to speak ill of others because it's easier than being loving and kind.

In Titus 3:2, we are told 'to speak evil of no one' and 'to show every courtesy to everyone'. Of course it's easy to love our neighbour when our neighbour is kind, caring and easy to get along with. But the people in our lives who are hard to love are often the ones who need love the most. Maybe my annoying colleague is dealing with a difficult personal situation. Maybe the neighbour with the barking dog is working at a second job because of financial problems.

We are commanded by God to love, not to judge. Thankfully, God knows we are imperfect and forgives us when we fail to speak lovingly to others. All we can do is to keep trying and keep praying for strength to succeed in speaking lovingly to and about everyone.

Prayer: *O Lord, help us have only kind words for others as we remember how you love us. Amen*

Thought for the day: 'Be kind to one another, tenderhearted, forgiving one another' (Ephesians 4:32).

April Rowland (Missouri, US)

God walks with us

Read Exodus 13:17–22

The Lord makes firm the steps of the one who delights in him.
Psalm 37:23 (NIV)

Several years ago I participated in a pilgrimage to the Holy Land. In Jordan, I visited the city of Petra. I had the opportunity to walk alongside our guide, a Bedouin nomad. During our time together I asked him if he had a certain approach to or strategy for walking in the desert. He did not immediately reply. Instead he stopped, picked up a stone and hurled it several yards ahead of us. He began to walk again and motioned for me to accompany him. When we reached the spot where the stone landed, he picked it up and hurled it once more. He smiled and said, 'I walk in the desert from stone to stone.'

That evening as I read *El Aposento Alto*, the Spanish language edition of *The Upper Room*, I understood the guide's message in a new way. Life is lived in stages. It is a journey of diverse experiences: trials, disappointments, achievements and so on. By asking God to walk with us, we can face life's most challenging experiences and live one 'stone' at a time.

Prayer: *Thank you, dear God, for walking beside us every day. You are our guide, in good times and in bad times. Amen*

Thought for the day: God walks beside me every day.

Pedro M. Mayol (Puerto Rico)

Foggy faith

Read 2 Kings 6:8–17

Elisha prayed, 'Lord, please open his eyes that he may see.' Then the Lord opened the servant's eyes, and he saw that the mountain was full of horses and fiery chariots surrounding Elisha.

2 Kings 6:17 (CEB)

I awakened to a fog-filled morning. The fog had crept in while I slept, shrouding my neighbourhood and reducing visibility. Peering out of my front window, I couldn't see my neighbour's house, just 25 feet in front of me. It wasn't until three hours later, when the fog lifted, that the house became visible again.

Sometimes I feel as if my life is shrouded in fog. In the midst of uncertainty, loss or a broken relationship I have trouble seeing my heavenly Father's face, even though I know that he is always near.

Elisha's servant also suffered from 'foggy' faith. He awoke to find an army of enemy chariots surrounding the city. Seeing himself in danger of being killed or captured, the servant panicked. Elisha, however, wasn't fooled. He knew that God and his angels were also there. 'Help him see,' Elisha prayed. Suddenly the servant's eyes were opened, and he could see the help that had been there all along.

God is always near, even when our circumstances make it difficult to see the help that is available to us.

Prayer: *Dear Lord, help us to see beyond the difficulties we are experiencing to realise that you are at work. Thank you for your constant presence. Amen*

Thought for the day: Though I cannot see God with my eyes, I know that he is always near.

Lori Hatcher (South Carolina, US)

Time to rest

Read Ecclesiastes 3:9–14

I know that there is nothing better for people than to be happy and to do good.
Ecclesiastes 3:12 (NIV)

I enjoy spending time with my daughter, but we both lead busy lives and don't get together as often as we'd like. As my 69th birthday approached, she asked 'Isn't it time for you to retire? Then we could see each other more often. Wouldn't you like to slow down and rest?'

I've considered retiring. Some days I really don't feel like going to my four-day-a-week job at the retirement home. Working with residents who have dementia is sometimes stressful, and the thought of not going to work is appealing. I lie in bed for that extra ten minutes and think, 'When I retire, I'll sleep as late as I want to.'

However, I worry that I'll get bored at home. Heaven knows my house needs a good clean, but a person can do only so much cleaning and organising. But then I think about the Bible study I lead for residents and about the staff I mentor. I may be turning 69, but I'm still useful.

That's when I remember to thank the Lord for giving me the energy to continue working and to keep on making a difference. When it's time for me to retire, I trust that God will give me something else to do. As long as we have breath, God has a purpose for us. In the meantime, I will rest in the knowledge that he has plans to prosper me and not to harm me, plans to give me hope and a future (see Jeremiah 29:11).

Prayer: *Heavenly Father, help us to work happily in the place you have called us. Guide us so that we may serve others as long as we have breath. Amen*

Thought for the day: As long I have breath, God has a purpose for me.

Diana L. Walters (Tennessee, US)

Provision

Read Psalm 147:4–11

[Jesus said], 'Look at the birds of the air; they do not sow or reap or store away in barns, and yet your heavenly Father feeds them. Are you not much more valuable than they?'
Matthew 6:26 (NIV)

The stretch of river near our home rarely freezes, even in the coldest weather. The running water attracts large numbers of migratory waterfowl to stay during the cold season. Each day, my wife takes food to these ducks and geese. At first the birds were cautious and wary, but now these beautiful, graceful animals recognise my wife and her bucket of food. They crowd around her to be fed.

This scene reminds me to give thanks for God's provision. All that we have – our talents, abilities and knowledge – are gifts from him. When we use them to serve him, we may find that our needs are met or exceeded. When we find ourselves with an abundance we can share this with others, recognising God as the source of all good things.

God is present in our world and in our lives. Just as the birds flock to my wife for food, we can go to him in joyous expectation of the love and provision promised to us.

Prayer: *Dear God, open our eyes to see and our ears to hear. Help us to recognise you as the source of good in the world and in our lives. Guide us to use these good provisions to serve you. Amen*

Thought for the day: How can I share God's unending love with others today?

Gale A. Richards (Iowa, US)

'How, God?'

Read Numbers 11:10–23

The Lord answered Moses, 'Is the Lord's arm too short? Now you will see whether or not what I say will come true for you.'
Numbers 11:23 (NIV)

God had promised to give the Israelites meat which they would eat for a whole month, even though they were deep in the wilderness. Wondering how God would pull this off, Moses voiced his doubts to him.

The questions Moses asked remind me of questions I have asked God. How on earth can God sort out the clutter in my life? How can he help with my debt or provide for me when I have no income? How will he sort out my dysfunctional family? How on earth, God, are you going to pull this off?

When I read God's answer to Moses it seems relevant to my struggles today. I imagine God asking me, 'Have I become a human being that you think you can limit me? Has my ability become inadequate? Am I no longer God? Why are you worried about how I will do what I have said?'

We do not need to worry about how God will care for us or remain faithful. When we remember Moses' story, we can rest assured that as surely as meat came to the Israelites, God will hear our prayers and answer us as well.

Prayer: *Dear God, help us to trust in your loving care and turn our worries over to you. Amen*

Thought for the day: I will leave my worries at the foot of the cross.

Lilian Nwanze Akobo (Ireland)

Palm Sunday

Read John 15:12–13

Greater love has no one than this: to lay down one's life for one's friends.
John 15:13 (NIV)

Recently, our children, Sophie and Aidan, had the opportunity to experience tubing. This involves riding on an inflated tube pulled by a long rope attached to the back of a speedboat.

Aidan was first to accept the challenge. He held on tightly as the tube skidded across the lake. After the ride he encouraged Sophie to join him. Both boarded the tube, and the boat picked up speed. Suddenly Aidan slipped off the tube and splashed into the water.

Later Aidan told me that he had let go of the tube on purpose because Sophie was getting scared. He knew the driver would stop the boat if he slid off.

I was impressed that Aidan gave up his sense of security for the sake of his sister. Sacrifice is a noble act that extends far beyond a story of two children on a lake. But Aidan's actions helped me to think more deeply about the meaning of sacrifice. Jesus made the ultimate sacrifice for each of us; he gave up his life so that we might live. When we see others make small sacrifices, we can remember Jesus. Letting go so that someone else can hang on changes the world!

Prayer: *Dear Jesus, thank you for the sacrifice you made for us on the cross to save us from our sins. In your name we pray. Amen*

Thought for the day: Jesus made the ultimate sacrifice for me.

Chuck Kralik (Missouri, US)

PRAYER FOCUS: SOMEONE WHO SACRIFICES FOR OTHERS

Motives

Read Mark 10:35–52

[Jesus asked], 'What do you want me to do for you?'
Mark 10: 36, 51 (NIV)

James and John, who had been with Jesus throughout his ministry, were seeking status and privilege for themselves, asking self-importantly for places of favour in his kingdom. They came to Jesus with what amounted to a command. Understandably their arrogance sparked indignation from their fellow disciples. Perhaps Jesus was disappointed by how little they had learned, as he taught them again the importance of developing a servant heart.

Bartimaeus, on the other hand, had never been near Jesus before. He was only a blind beggar, sitting on the edge of Jericho where travellers came and went. When he cried out, 'Jesus, Son of David, have mercy on me!' many in the crowd around Jesus told him roughly to be quiet. But Jesus heard him, stopped and had him brought forward. He asked, 'What do you want me to do for you?'

In sharp contrast to the two disciples, Bartimaeus spoke humbly out of his deepest need, asking for a life-changing miracle. What he had already heard others saying about Jesus gave Bartimaeus the confidence to ask for the one thing only Jesus could give him.

Jesus asked the same question on both occasions, knowing already what was in each person's heart and mind. The disciples received a chastening lesson; Bartimaeus received his sight and a new-found faith. I pray that I will, like Bartimaeus, pray to Jesus with a humble heart.

Prayer: *Lord, open my eyes to see and understand your ways, and to choose your way forward for my life. Amen*

Thought for the day: Our motives matter to Jesus.

Hazel Thompson (Somerset, England)

Life-fulfilling purpose

Read Matthew 6:25–34

Do not worry about your life, what you will eat or drink; or about your body, what you will wear. Is not life more than food, and the body more than clothes?
Matthew 6:25 (NIV)

On the day my class graduated from college I broke down in tears. Between sobs, I wished I could celebrate with my friends as we embarked on the next great adventure of life together. Instead, I was alone in a maximum-security prison, the cold walls and bars shrouding me in darkness.

In prison I believed that my life was over. God, however, proved otherwise when an in-prison Bible college was established. Now I am privileged to study there and share the gospel with other inmates. In the Sermon on the Mount, Jesus tells us to set aside our worries and give attention to more important issues of life, such as seeking God's kingdom and righteousness (Matthew 6:33). In my new life, I have been able to do that.

At times we all may worry that we are living wasted lives. What we fail to realise, though, is that these worries are wasting countless hours of our lives. No matter where we find ourselves, when we set our worries aside and focus on God we can find a life-fulfilling purpose.

Prayer: *Dear Lord Jesus, help me to focus more on you and less on myself.*

Thought for the day: Energy I spend worrying could be used to fulfil God's purpose for me.

Brandon B. Brewer (Texas, US)

Jesus never fails

Read 1 Kings 19:1–9

Even before a word is on my tongue, O Lord, you know it completely.
Psalm 139:4 (NRSV)

I was at my best friend's home feeling anxious and fed-up because I had been facing difficulties related to my job. My friend was at work, but her children and her mother were of great comfort to me. They were a delight to be with. They showered me with love as they loaded me up with sweets, paintings, small craft items they had made and some books by my favourite Christian authors. Over a cup of hot tea my friend's mum and I read from the Bible and prayed together.

This time with my friends reminded me of when Elijah fled from wicked Queen Jezebel, only to have God minister to him through an angel who provided him sustenance. The Bible tells us in Psalm 46 that God is mighty, a strong fortress for us. As our rock, God is concerned with every small detail of our lives.

I left my friends that day rejoicing. I did not have a solution to my work problem, but I felt reassured that the answer was on the way.

Prayer: *O Lord, we give thanks to you for your everlasting love. If calamity comes upon us, remind us to call on you, knowing that you will hear us. Amen*

Thought for the day: When anxiety threatens to overwhelm me, God offers peace.

Anitha Eliet (Tamil Nadu, India)

A gift of life

Read John 3:16–21
Love your neighbour as yourself.
Mark 12:31 (NRSV)

I recently received what I call a gift of life. I do not yet know where it came from, and I may never know, but it has freed me from many impairments, both physical and emotional. It has given me hope and a chance for renewed life.

What was the gift? An organ donor gave me a kidney that was matched with my own. I am sure such gifts are given every day; but it was a miracle to me, and I am truly grateful for God's grace.

I think of another miracle that is the gift of life: 'God so loved the world that he gave his only Son.' With this gift of God's deep love for us we received freedom from transgressions and the promise of eternal life. We must not pass Calvary and think it's just a hill. It is the source of our hope and truly a gift of life – both here and for eternity.

I have been blessed. We have all been blessed by the grace of God.

Prayer: *Our Father, may we always be mindful of the gifts of life you have given us. We pray as Jesus taught us, saying, 'Our Father in heaven, hallowed be your name, your kingdom come, your will be done on earth as it is in heaven. Give us today our daily bread. Forgive us our debts, as we also have forgiven our debtors. And lead us not into temptation, but deliver us from the evil one.'* Amen*

Thought for the day: I can be an instrument of God's grace to others.

William Kline (California, US)

PRAYER FOCUS: ORGAN DONORS AND RECIPIENTS
*Matthew 6:9–13, NIV

Good Friday

Read Luke 23:32–43
Jesus said, 'Father, forgive them, for they don't know what they're doing.'
Luke 23:34 (CEB)

It's morning and the school is quiet, but there are some pupils walking in a procession to their classrooms. I walk with unsteady steps to mine. Some boys mock me. They imitate the way I walk and taunt me. 'Cripple, are you going to school? Can you? Look at how she's walking! Walk faster, cripple! You'll be late for school!' All I can do is cry.

After 40 years, remembering that incident still brings pain to my heart. But every time I read the story of Jesus' crucifixion, my pain gradually diminishes. The harsh words about my disability are nothing compared to what Jesus had to face. Jesus was mocked and whipped, given a crown of thorns and crucified. Through all this, he never sought revenge. Instead, he prayed that God would forgive the people who tortured and killed him.

Jesus' forgiveness is an example for all of us. He showed the power of forgiveness that wipes away revenge, anger and pain.

The new life we experience by forgiving others as Jesus forgives us is what Easter means to me.

Prayer: *Dear Saviour, teach us to follow your example in forgiving others so that we can share your joy, love and peace with others this Easter. Amen*

Thought for the day: I will follow Jesus' example and seek to forgive someone who has hurt me.

Lautan Asima Basaria Siregar (Jakarta, Indonesia)

The Saviour knows

Read Matthew 27:45–56

Jesus said, 'Come to me, all you that are weary and are carrying heavy burdens, and I will give you rest. Take my yoke upon you... and you will find rest for your souls. For my yoke is easy, and my burden is light.'
Matthew 11:28–30 (NRSV)

I have been in prison for more than 19 years, and sometimes I think that nobody understands the brokenness and loneliness I experience. In those times, I remind myself what Jesus went through, and I know that he understands my pain. He came to the world to be one of us, taking flesh upon himself to redeem the world. And yet, he was crucified.

Jesus knows what it is to hurt, both physically and emotionally. He knows what it is to suffer betrayal, to be pushed away and be forsaken by those he loves. He understands all the pain that I am going through.

But Jesus' story didn't end with the pain of the crucifixion. After the cross came the resurrection. Jesus rose from the grave to conquer death. He sits at the right hand of God now, and he still reaches out to the broken and weary. I put myself in his hands because I know he is able to heal my broken heart and to bind up my wounds.

Prayer: *Dear Lord, help us to remember that you understand our difficulties and that you promise to heal our brokenness when we turn to you. Amen*

Thought for the day: Jesus loves the lonely and heals those who hurt.

R. Aaron Flaherty (Texas, US)

Easter Sunday

Read Philippians 3:7–11

I am the Living One; I was dead, and now look, I am alive for ever and ever!
Revelation 1:18 (NIV)

I love to sit in my back garden and look out over the lake. When the sun is shining, the lake sparkles and dances in the light. But on that Easter morning the fog covered the lake like a thick grey blanket undulating across the water. But as the sun rose and warmed the air, the fog began to thin out and move away – leaving the lake shimmering in the beautiful bright sunlight again. No match for the intense heat of the rising sun, the thick blanket of fog had disappeared.

I thought how appropriate this was for Easter morning. Because Jesus rose to give us life, the fog has been lifted from our lives, and we are able to see him in all his risen glory. And because Jesus lives within us, we can be a light to others.

The darkness of sin and death was defeated as the stone rolled away on Easter morning. Just as the fog that morning had no power to overcome the heat of the rising sun, sin and death have no power to overcome the love and salvation of God through Christ. Jesus is risen! Alleluia!

Prayer: *Thank you, almighty God, for the hope that Easter holds for each of us. Help us to share this hope with others. In the name of the risen Christ. Amen*

Thought for the day: Jesus' resurrection gives hope to the world.

Linda Fasking (Kentucky, US)

Sunrise

Read Matthew 28:1–10

Jesus came and spake unto them, saying, All power is given unto me in heaven and in earth.
Matthew 28:18 (KJV)

All Jesus' promises were forgotten as his disciples wept through the darkness of sorrow, doubt and fear after the crucifixion of their friend and teacher.

But at sunrise, on the first day of the week, everything changed. The women got up and walked to the tomb. The angel rolled away the stone. The light of the sunrise revealed the empty tomb, and the women ran to share the news of their risen Saviour. In doing so, they met Jesus.

With the sunrise came Jesus' voice: 'Be not afraid: go tell my brethren that they go into Galilee, and there shall they see me' (Matthew 28:10, KJV). When Jesus arrived, he did not scold the disciples for doubting him. Instead Jesus reminded them that he is the source of all power.

Sunrise brought the dawning of redemption that day. This redemption continues to be our hope today when we trudge through the dark and lonely valleys of pain and sorrow in our lives. The sunrise may bring healing for a broken marriage or for a body broken with disease. God, who rolled away the stone from the vacant tomb that morning long ago, has the power to make all things new.

Prayer: *Dear God, when we struggle through pain and sorrow, help us to have hope and faith that the sun will rise. Amen*

Thought for the day: This Easter season, I can look forward to the dawn of redemption.

Sharon Finch O'Maley (Texas, US)

PRAYER FOCUS: TO FIND HOPE IN THE RESURRECTION

Not growing weary

Read Psalm 119:25–32

My soul clings to the dust; revive me according to your word.
Psalm 119:25 (NRSV)

I remember a time when my body, mind and spirit were completely drained. My mother had recently passed away; our church was experiencing some serious leadership issues, and my son's hereditary illness flared up. Some of these events were sudden, but others had lingered for many months. I went about my daily life, automatically putting one foot in front of the other. Life felt like drudgery, and I ploughed through it painfully.

For some of us, weariness seems to be a way of life. I found my antidote to weariness in two places: in trusting that God would revive me and in serving others in tangible ways. I vowed to spend more time meditating on the Psalms, and I began to mentor a young man who had serious family problems. Soon my spirit was revived and my soul was nurtured.

I've seen that God often provides relief from our weariness as we focus on him, not on what we expect to receive. God can shift our focus away from our problems and toward helping those who are also struggling – bringing peace to others and to ourselves.

Prayer: *Dear Lord Jesus, renew us with your peace as we face challenges. Fill us with a desire to serve others. Amen*

Thought for the day: Trusting in God and serving others can revive my spirit.

Gary A. Miller (California, US)

How much longer?

Read 1 John 4:19–21

Let us not become weary in doing good, for at the proper time we will reap a harvest if we do not give up.
Galatians 6:9 (NIV)

I am a divorced woman with no children. You might think I have a lot of free time, but I have been taking care of my sister for 41 years. She has schizophrenia, and has to take regular medication in order to stabilise her mood.

Over the years, I have struggled alongside my sister as she has battled her illness. When she has recurrences of mania or depression, I have to seek help from her psychiatrist to make sure her medication is appropriate. When her temper flares, I have to bear with her – secretly praying for her to calm down. Although I often do not enjoy this work, my sister has brought me closer to the Lord because of my constant prayers for help.

Here in Thailand, there are no institutions where people living with mental illness can be cared for indefinitely. So I have asked God, 'Do I have the responsibility to take care of my sister for the rest of my life?' His answer has been that I am to care patiently for my sister for as long as I can. Therefore, if God puts me in this place and calls me to help my sister, I will gladly do so.

Prayer: *Helper of the weak, thank you for giving us the wisdom and patience to care for our loved ones. May we become your strength and peace for their lives. Amen*

Thought for the day: The Lord gives me strength to help others.

Doris Yeung (Samut Prakan, Thailand)

Three-legged race

Read Isaiah 49:13–18

The Lord said, 'Even [a woman] may forget [her nursing child], yet I will not forget you. See, I have inscribed you on the palms of my hands.'
Isaiah 49:15–16 (NRSV)

At the school sports day my younger brother and I tied a rope around my right ankle and his left ankle. Amid giggles we hobbled and swayed to the starting line.

'On your marks, get set, go!' We somehow managed to synchronise our strides and crossed the finish line first. Smiling widely, I looked over at all the parents, but no eyes or cameras were aimed our way. I thought, 'We won, so why isn't anyone looking at us or cheering for us? Doesn't anybody care about us?' All the parents' eyes were glued on their own children, and my brother and I had no parents to applaud us. They had both died a few years earlier.

Since then, today's verse has taught me that I have always had and will always have a heavenly Father who loves and approves of me. I realised that my thought that I had no parent applauding me was wrong. God, our heavenly parent, is always watching us and cheering us on.

Prayer: *Heavenly Father, remind us, especially those of us who do not have earthly parents, that we all have you. Amen*

Thought for the day: With God, I am never alone, abandoned or forgotten.

Jim Good (Ohio, US)

God's word helps us

Read Psalm 119:10–16

I treasure your word in my heart, so that I may not sin against you.
Psalm 119:11 (NRSV)

It has always been easy for me to get into debates with friends and family, and I find myself arguing more than I should. If I make others angry, I regret it, and I'm always willing to apologise and move on. I just can't pass up a rousing exchange of ideas about current events.

I was like this for many years until one day, in the middle of a debate with my father that had turned into an argument, I suddenly forgot what I was going to say. The only thing I could remember was today's quoted verse. It was the verse from my Bible study a few weeks before. In an instant, my perspective changed. I realised I was so caught up in the conversation that I was about to say something hurtful to my father just to 'win' the argument. I held my tongue that day and we called a truce.

Later on, I thanked God for bringing that verse to my mind at just the right time. The more we read and study God's word, the more we are able to draw on its direction when we need it.

Prayer: *Thank you, dear God, for giving us wisdom through scripture when we need it most. Amen*

Thought for the day: Before speaking, I will pray for God's wisdom.

Pamela L. Dorrel (Kentucky, US)

Lean on me

Read Exodus 17:8–16

When Moses' hands grew tired... Aaron and Hur held his hands up – one on one side, one on the other – so that his hands remained steady till sunset.
Exodus 17:12 (NIV)

I grew up on a farm where hard work was the norm. Muscles became cramped and chores seemed endless. When we needed a break, we often leaned against the closest fence. It propped us up while we drank cold water, wiped our faces and wondered how much longer it was until it was time to stop for the day.

Just like those fences, good friends support us during trying times. We can depend on them always to be there – firm, steadfast, secure.

That's what Aaron and Hur did for Moses. When Moses grew weary, they held up his hands so that they 'remained steady till sunset'. They stayed with him, never wavering, until he completed his task of making sure the Israelites were victorious.

Examples like these and other men and women of the Bible prompt me to ask, 'Do I allow others to lean on me when they're weak?' As God's family we can ask ourselves, 'Do we offer a place for people to catch their breath before they move on? Do we provide a moment of respite when they think their task will never end?' We can resolve to prop one another up when life gets tough.

As we are there to prop up those around us, we can rely on God's strength to support us when life gets tough.

Prayer: *Dear God, help us be vessels of your strength as we extend our hands in support of one another. Amen*

Thought for the day: God gives us hands to meet others' needs.

Diana C. Derringer (Kentucky, US)

Guidance and direction

Read Psalm 119:97–106

All Scripture is God-breathed and is useful for teaching, rebuking, correcting and training in righteousness, so that the servant of God may be thoroughly equipped for every good work.
2 Timothy 3:16–17 (NIV)

In 2014 our family migrated from Pakistan to Canada. As newcomers, we faced many challenges during the initial months. One of these was to learn our way around our new city. One day we needed to go to the local school to arrange our younger son's admission. We checked the directions before driving, but somehow we took a wrong turn and went in a different direction. We were very upset when we discovered how far away from the school we had ended up.

My elder son suggested we get a sat nav system to help us find our way while driving. That same day we bought one and started using it. We just had to type in the address and follow the directions to reach a destination.

This experience led me to think about our life as faithful Christians. We are all on a journey toward eternal life, and the Bible serves as our 'sat nav' – providing guidance and direction for moving closer to God. During this journey, if we read and follow the teachings of scripture, we can move closer and closer to our ultimate destination: eternal life.

Prayer: *Thank you, dear Lord, for scripture which guides us in your way in this life and toward life eternal. Amen*

Thought for the day: Following God's word is the best way to navigate life.

Zafar Iqbal (Ontario, Canada)

Peace in the storm

Read Luke 8:22–25

Jesus said to his disciples, 'Peace I leave with you; my peace I give you. I do not give to you as the world gives. Do not let your hearts be troubled and do not be afraid.'
John 14:27 (NIV)

God, please help me! My father had just passed away and I was on an emotional roller coaster. One minute I was coping and the next I was in a deep pit of anguish and despair. I realised that now was the time to pray for God's peace that passes all understanding (see Philippians 4:7). When I returned home, I talked to my neighbour about my struggle. She gently reminded me of the peace that God so readily gives, and offered to pray for peace for me. This experience helped me to realise that God's peace would get me through this time in my life.

Although I still miss my father greatly, I know that I am not alone in the midst of my anguish. God gives me the strength and peace to carry me through any storm.

We face many storms in life. At times, it feels as if the pain is so deep that it will overwhelm us. We may feel alone in the depths of our despair. However, God has promised never to leave us or forsake us. When we pray in the midst of the storm, God will grant us the peace that passes all understanding.

Prayer: *Dear heavenly Father, thank you for always being there for us. In Jesus' name. Amen*

Thought for the day: I am never alone because God has promised never to leave me.

Jodi Wheeler (Arizona, US)

Simple joys

Read Lamentations 3:21–25

Make a joyful noise to the Lord, all the earth. Worship the Lord with gladness; come into his presence with singing.
Psalm 100:1–2 (NRSV)

Our two-year-old grandson, Gabriel, is a delight to all his family. My husband and I are in our 70s and our other two grandchildren are teenagers, so it has been a blessing to us all to have this little one come into our lives.

Gabriel greets every morning with great enthusiasm, looks at all his toys as if they are brand new and gives everyone hugs and kisses as if they have been away for a long time. He inspects everything outside – leaves, pebbles, flowers, insects – as if he had not seen them just the day before.

What if we all appreciated each new day with the same excitement? What if we were as joyful and loving as Gabriel? What if we thanked God for our blessings instead of dwelling on unpleasantness? Perhaps our enthusiasm about our love of God and our faith would be clear to others. How wonderful it would be if our joy in our faith was passed on to just one person, making that person want to experience the fullness of knowing God!

Prayer: *Dear God, help us to greet with enthusiasm the blessings you give us through the simple pleasures of your handiwork. Help us to share our faith in you with others. In Jesus' name, we pray. Amen*

Thought for the day: What excites me about my faith in Christ?

Patricia Steagall (North Carolina, US)

PRAYER FOCUS: TO SHARE THE JOY OF KNOWING GOD

Show me the way

Read Psalm 16:1–11

Always be prepared to give an answer to everyone who asks you to give the reason for the hope that you have. But do this with gentleness and respect.
1 Peter 3:15 (NIV)

Before I came to faith in Christ, I was hopeless and without joy. I knew I did things that were wrong, but I was unable to see how I could change my life for the better. Then I met some people at my high school who seemed to have something special: their lives were different and meaningful. As I watched them, I realised that they weren't just happy, they were joyful. That was strange to me yet also very appealing. I asked them many questions and appreciated their kind responses.

When people ask me how I became a Christian, I always point to the significant impact of those joyful Christians who demonstrated purposeful living in God's presence. No matter what difficulties they faced in life, they truly praised God. They even thought it was important to share this response with me, letting me know that the path of true life and everlasting joy can be found only in Jesus. I give thanks for their joyfulness that showed me the way to new life in Christ.

Prayer: *Dear Lord, you alone are our greatest joy. Thank you for giving us new life in Jesus Christ. Amen*

Thought for the day: I can show my joy in the Lord to the people around me.

Mike Medeiros (California, US)

A better way

Read 2 Corinthians 12:6–10

[The Lord] said to [Paul], 'My grace is sufficient for you, for my power is made perfect in weakness.'
2 Corinthians 12:9 (NIV)

At times, when I look at my commitments for the weeks ahead, I wonder how I can possibly fit everything in. At other times I worry about how I will manage to cope with all of life's challenges. At these times I can choose to become anxious and think about the worst-case scenarios, or I can choose a different way. I can stop worrying and start praying. Usually prayer calms me – reminding me to trust God one day at a time. His grace is sufficient for each moment of each day (see 2 Corinthians 12:6–9). I can choose to trust in God's strength and be thankful even for my weaknesses. I can choose to live in the present and open my eyes and ears to enjoy the blessings of each day instead of worrying about tomorrow and the next challenge. I can choose to take negative thoughts captive (see 2 Corinthians 10:5) and think instead on the truth in God's word.

I cannot say that I always find it easy to do this, but with practice it has gradually become the norm for me. From experience, I know that I can trust God to meet all my needs. I've seen him give me strength exactly when I need it. So I choose a better way to live – one day at a time – confidently relying on God with a thankful heart.

Prayer: *Loving Father, give us confidence to trust you in every situation. In the challenges of life, help us to rely on your strength, not our own. Amen*

Thought for the day: Today I will stop worrying and start praying.

Ann Stewart (South Australia, Australia)

The Spirit's voice

Read Luke 11:9–13

Jesus said, 'I will ask the Father, and he will give you another Advocate, to be with you for ever. This is the Spirit of truth.'
John 14:16–17 (NRSV)

The divisions at our church's annual meeting mirrored the divisions in my own household. I saw good people on both sides of contentious issues.

A few days after the church meeting, I took my son to hear a performance of his favourite work, Mahler's 3rd Symphony. On the heels of the tension we had both experienced, the music became a visceral reminder of the Holy Spirit's still, small voice. In one of the later movements of Mahler's work, the principal trumpet was offstage, barely audible at times, but supplying the main theme for the piece – a sweet, longing melody calling to all who would listen. At times, some of the other instruments picked up on the trumpet's gentle theme and harmonised with it; at other times they almost drowned it out in a frenzy of dissonant notes.

I wondered, 'Which kind of instrument am I?' At times, I am so eager to voice my own opinions and positions that I nearly drown out God's Spirit of truth, not to mention other people's voices. But when I calm down enough to listen, that Spirit is still there, singing softly and tenderly. In fact, the Spirit is sometimes echoed by those I may be trying to outmanoeuvre verbally. Becoming an instrument of peace starts with listening for the Holy Spirit.

Prayer: *Gracious God, thank you for sending your Holy Spirit to us. Give us ears to hear your truth and hearts to understand. In the name of Jesus. Amen*

Thought for the day: I can find peace when I listen for the Holy Spirit.

Anne Kayser (Oregon, US)

Light in the darkness

Read John 1:1–13
You are the light of the world.
Matthew 5:14 (NIV)

I lay down my book. Childhood memories flooded my mind. The paragraph I had been reading told of an old lamplighter, and in a mist of recollection I recalled a shadowy figure who visited our street. He came every evening at dusk and, standing beside the lamp at our gate, he would lift a long pole up to the gas lantern. A pool of light would spill across our Victorian pathway and our world would be bathed in light. It seemed like a miracle. I was amazed that I had remembered this scene from years ago.

To a child, I suppose those strings of twinkling lights were both magical and memorable. But more impressive still is the memory of lights shining in the darkness, one after another like a chain of Chinese whispers, until every city street-light was lit.

As my mind dwelled on lights in the darkness, I thought about our faith. Every time we speak about our faith, it is akin to a lamp being lit. Every word lights a spark, and from that spark comes the great light of revelation. Jesus said, 'You are the light of the world.' May the light of our personal testimony shine brightly for him.

Prayer: *Lord, may we shine brightly in the world for you. Amen*

Thought for the day: Our personal testimony can be a source of light for others.

Pauline Pullan (Yorkshire, England)

PRAYER FOCUS: TO BRING LIGHT INTO DARK PLACES

God's goodness

Read Psalm 27:1–14

I remain confident of this: I will see the goodness of the Lord in the land of the living.
Psalm 27:13 (NIV)

In 2013 my husband suffered a heart attack that left him with a heart function of only 30%, and he was given a pacemaker. It felt like a miracle that he was able to overcome this and other related physical challenges. Ever since that experience, Psalm 27:13 has become one of my favourite passages of scripture.

Early in 2016, my husband's health suffered another setback caused by renal complications. He endured difficult days with much pain. Yet still, we saw God's goodness. Later when my husband died, it was difficult to see death as part of God's goodness. We – my husband's family and friends – experienced moments when we lacked understanding, but God remained faithful. Accepting his goodness allowed us the grace to see the fullness of his promise with faith and hope, the promise of life eternal without illness, pain or anguish.

Prayer: *God of hope, thank you for surrounding us with your strength, love and goodness even in our sadness. With the psalmist we remain confident that we will see your goodness. Amen*

Thought for the day: God's goodness can be found in every situation.

Ircha Martinez (Puerto Rico)

Through the Father's eyes

Read Romans 8:12–17

You received a Spirit that shows you are adopted as [God's] children. With this Spirit, we cry, 'Abba, Father.'
Romans 8:15 (CEB)

Nine years ago when I held my first-born child, Melina, for the first time, I knew I had what had been missing in my life. I knew that there in that hospital with Melina, I was exactly where God wanted me to be. Now with five wonderful children, four girls and one boy, I can see myself in them: in my son David's protective instinct, in Melina's creativity and sense of humour, in Serena's feisty spirit, in Ellie's need for hugs, in Faith's silliness. Yet, when we are together in public, people often stare at us, probably because my children are Hispanic and I am not; all of them are adopted.

When I look at my children, all I see is Melina, Ellie, David, Serena and Faith. They are the joy of my life. I often smile when I remember that the way I see my children is the way God sees each of us; he delights in us. No matter what our experience with earthly fathers is, having God as our parent means that we have access to safety, love, guidance, help, courage and security. The apostle Paul reminds us of this personal, loving relationship we can have with God in today's quoted verse. As God's children, we find our identity and our home.

Prayer: *Abba, Father, thank you for adopting us into your family. Help us to love you and to extend your love to others. Amen*

Thought for the day: Because we are God's children, we always have a home.

Stephen Johnson (California, US)

Every good thing

Read Psalm 34:4–10

Taste and see that the Lord is good; blessed is the one who takes refuge in him… Those who fear him lack nothing… Those who seek the Lord lack no good thing.
Psalm 34:8–10 (NIV)

Over the years, my neighbourhood has become home to a rather large stray-cat population. Several of us within the community provide clean drinking water and fresh food for these cats daily so they're well fed and not tearing apart everyone's rubbish bags in search of a meal.

It has worked well, with the exception of one cat we call Smokey. Though I've seen Smokey eating from various food bowls often enough, he continues to tear through rubbish bags and to drink dirty water from gutters and puddles.

Once, in frustration, as I caught him feasting from a neighbour's rubbish, I yelled out, 'Smokey! Why are you messing with that when I've got something so much better for you here?' Not long afterward, I wondered to myself how many times God has asked me that very same question.

God has so much better to offer us – the best there is! In Psalm 34:8, we're invited to 'taste and see that the Lord is good'. Yet for various reasons we keep picking through life's rubbish. Maybe it's time to leave that where it belongs and joyfully come to the table where God has every good thing waiting for us.

Prayer: *Faithful God, help us joyfully to receive every good thing you have prepared for us. Amen*

Thought for the day: God offers me the best; I only have to accept it.

Pam Manners (New Jersey, US)

Called by name

Read John 10:1–5

The Lord says, 'I have called you by name; you are mine.'
Isaiah 43:1 (CEB)

The day's news brought another image of refugees. I had seen many scenes of distraught people huddled together on their perilous sea journey or their long march to safety and new life. This time it was an image of a crowd pressing against an impassable razor-wire fence. Then, over the commentator's voice I heard someone call, 'Zaria!' Suddenly I no longer saw a crowd but a group of individual people. Like Zaria, each one has their own personal story, their own experiences of horror, fear, loss, pain and sacrifice, their own hopes, faith and loves.

Jesus taught us that while God's love is for the whole world it is also very personal. In today's reading Jesus likened God to the perfect shepherd who knows each sheep by name. God will suffer for and with each to ensure that no one is lost.

From that day on, my prayers have changed. I no longer pray, 'Lord, help refugees', but 'Lord, take into your loving care Zaria and every other refugee and asylum-seeker like her.' No longer do my prayers come from impersonal concern, but from intimate compassion – closer to the way God loves each of us.

Prayer: *Dear Lord Jesus Christ, give us your compassion to share the pain and joy of individuals in a crowded world of injustice, until all our prayers are acts of love. Amen*

Thought for the day: Today I will pray for someone by name.

Colin Harbach (Cumbria, England)

Under construction

Read 2 Corinthians 4:8–18

Unless the Lord builds the house, those who build it labour in vain.
Psalm 127:1 (NRSV)

Our home has been under reconstruction for quite some time now, and we have taken down walls and ceilings. But many of the changes have been internal improvements that do not show, such as replacing pipes and electrical wiring. We know that the internal changes, although not seen, make for a better, stronger and safer home.

This reminds me of Paul in today's reading. He writes about being persecuted, afflicted and struck down, but not destroyed or forsaken, so that the invisible Christ within us – and the promise in his resurrection – can become visible to the world.

Ever since the day I claimed my faith in Christ, I also have been in a reconstruction period. Little by little, Christ has moulded, replaced and made new my spirit. Because he loves me enough to do this, I am able to hold up under the pressures of this world.

Reconstruction is hard, messy work. But the finished product will be well worth it all. If we are willing to let Christ renew us day by day – painful as it may be at times – we know that in the end we will become better, stronger and more effective witnesses. In God's care we can feel secure that he wants only good for us, not harm, and that we can look forward to a bright future with hope (see Jeremiah 29:11).

Prayer: *Dear Lord, help us not to fight the changes we need to make as we are transformed into Christ's image. In Jesus' name we pray. Amen*

Thought for the day: I can look forward to the way God will transform me.

Jenny Calvert (Texas, US)

A two-year-old's plea

Read Mark 9:35–37

Jesus said, 'Anyone who will not receive the kingdom of God like a little child will never enter it.'
Mark 10:15 (NIV)

I enjoy babysitting my granddaughter, Molly. But recently she had a high temperature and didn't feel well. An unhappy, poorly two-year-old can be a challenge! Yet Molly has taught me a lesson about God's love.

When Molly feels sad or stressed and needs comforting, she doesn't cry or demand to be held. She looks up at me and says, 'I need to hold you', as if I were the one who needed comforting! How could anyone resist a plea like that?

Our relationship with Jesus can be the same. Too often the only time we ask for Jesus' comforting arms is when we are in trouble. What we don't realise is that, like Molly, he is always saying to us, 'I need to hold you.' Jesus wants to hold us even when we don't realise it or think that we need him to. He wants to be our refuge and strength – and not just in times of trouble. How can we resist a plea like that?

We are all God's children. And, like Molly, we need to say to our heavenly Father, 'I need to hold you.' In Mark 10:16 we are assured of God's response: '[Jesus] took the children in his arms, placed his hands on them and blessed them' (NIV).

Prayer: *Dear Jesus, we want to feel the safety of your embrace. We need your loving arms around us today and every day. Amen*

Thought for the day: Fear and sadness cannot win when I am in God's arms.

Miles Q. Turner (Illinois, US)

Chorus of praise

Read Psalm 19:1–14

Say to God... All the earth worships you, sings praises to you, sings praises to your name!
Psalm 66:3–4 (CEB)

I love the early morning when it is still dark, but the pale light of dawn is beginning to show. I rise early and then I listen for the soft, lonely voice of the morning's first bird. Within a few seconds of the first birdsong, the voice of another bird joins in. A few seconds later a third joins, then ten, then a hundred, and then the myriad sounds of the dawn chorus fill the air.

At this time of day, when silence is broken by the first birds starting to praise God, I have a particularly strong sense of my Creator's presence, power and love. Each morning, this glorious sound inspires me anew to pray and worship him. The birds encourage me to lift my voice in praise for all of the ways God is faithful to me, for the beauty of creation and especially for these birds, which are the first heralds of God's power each morning.

Prayer: *O God, we thank you for the beauty of your creation, and for the first singing birds, from whom we learn to praise you every morning of every new day. Amen*

Thought for the day: 'I will awake the dawn. I will give thanks to you, O Lord' (Psalm 57:8–9, NRSV).

Alla Vuksta (Uzhgorod, Ukraine)

Looking forward

Read Luke 2:36–38

[We look] for that blessed hope, and the glorious appearing of the great God and our Saviour Jesus Christ.
Titus 2:13 (KJV)

Sometimes I find myself complaining about the aches and pains of old age and reminiscing about the 'good old days'. In today's reading, we meet Anna, an elderly widow who did not complain or dwell on the past. She was a prophetess in Jesus' time and her circumstances were difficult. Widowed early, she may have felt purposeless and destitute. But her focus was on serving God and on the coming of the Messiah. Her waiting was rewarded when she saw Jesus in the arms of his mother. She gave thanks to God for this blessed experience and passed on the good news of his birth to others.

Anna has set a good example for us to follow. Her life was focused on the Lord and the future. She was busily engaged in serving God. Likewise, we can be future-oriented as we serve our Lord. Reminiscing can be meaningful and the afflictions of old age are disconcerting, but we can continue to look forward to Jesus' promises for the future. Motivated by the hope that Jesus' promises instil within us, we can be busy about God's business – worshipping, witnessing and serving others – with an undaunted forward look.

Prayer: *God of encouragement, help us to take our eyes off our own difficulties and focus on your promises and future blessings for the world. Amen*

Thought for the day: No matter how old I am, I can focus on God's promises for the future.

Wayne Greenawalt, Jr (Illinois, US)

Our guidebook

Read John 1:1–5

[Lord,] Your word is a lamp before my feet and a light for my journey.
Psalm 119:105 (CEB)

One autumn, my husband and I hiked beneath Diamond Head crater in Hawaii. It was a strenuous climb filled with pitch-black tunnels, a spiral staircase, other steep stairs and a tight squeeze through a concrete bunker built during World War II. I had read the guidebook and brought a torch to show us the path through the dark. When the way was difficult, it took a lot of effort to keep going. It would have been much easier to give up. But if we had given up, we would have missed the magnificent view that awaited us.

Much like that hike, life events can make us fearful, stressed or exhausted. We may feel as if we are walking straight uphill or as if we are lost in a dark tunnel. Our situations can be so tight and constricted, we aren't sure we'll make it to the glorious view ahead.

Whenever circumstances threaten to undo me, I remember that hike in Hawaii. Because I had read the guidebook, I was prepared. I also remember that the psalmist said that God's word, our guidebook, is a light for our journey, and I open its pages. I want God's light for each step of my journey through life.

Prayer: *Dear God, thank you for being a light on our path during our times in the dark. Amen*

Thought for the day: The Bible is my guidebook.

Sandy Kirby Quandt (Texas, US)

Standing in confidence

Read 1 Samuel 17:31–47

So we can say with confidence, 'The Lord is my helper; I will not be afraid. What can anyone do to me?'
Hebrews 13:6 (NRSV)

In today's reading, the battle lines were drawn and the stakes were high. Freedom was the prize. The Philistines stood confidently with Goliath leading them. The Israelites were in a state of turmoil, dismayed and terrified – all except for one: David, the youngest of Jesse's sons. David had confidence in himself and knew that God was leading the Israelites. He had even greater confidence that God stood with him and would deliver him from the danger he was facing.

Each one of us will experience times in our lives when the odds seem to be stacked against us and we feel weak, vulnerable and afraid. But it's in these times that we can remember with confidence that we are not alone – God is with us and will see us through.

Prayer: *Dear God, when the odds are stacked against us help us to stand confidently, knowing that you are at our side. In Jesus' name we pray. Amen*

Thought for the day: Like David, I can be confident that God will see me through.

Mandy Slade (Somerset, England)

PRAYER FOCUS: SOMEONE STRUGGLING TO TRUST GOD

A priceless gift

Read John 6:25–35

Jesus said to them, 'I am the bread of life. Whoever comes to me will never be hungry, and whoever believes in me will never be thirsty.'
John 6:35 (NRSV)

My parents were great people, but when I was young they weren't Christians. They hadn't been brought up in Christian homes, and they had a lot of questions. Even so, my mother found a place to have me baptised, and my brother and I were taken regularly to Sunday school.

Mum later came to Christ after becoming acquainted with Eileen, who shared her love of music and literature and whose life was grounded in the Lord. Dad found his way to faith through early-morning coffee meetings with my caring minister, Reverend Zuhl, who helped my father confront his faith issues.

Reverend Zuhl and Eileen helped bring my family to unity in Christ and brought the bread of life to my spiritually hungry family. My mother eventually told me that her morning prayer always includes, 'Lord, put me in a place of need today.' And God has seldom disappointed her. Opportunities for ministry found her wherever she was. Our friends gave our family a priceless gift that we can all share with others – the joyful gift of God's love.

Prayer: *Dear Lord, give us an awareness of those around us who need to know Christ. May the joy we find in following you bring light to someone else's life today. In Jesus' name. Amen*

Thought for the day: With whom may I share Christ's life-giving bread today?

Betty Armstrong (Texas, US)

In tandem

Read Proverbs 3:5–10

Jeremiah wrote, 'Lord, I know that people's lives are not their own; it is not for them to direct their steps.'
Jeremiah 10:23 (NIV)

As a young couple, my husband and I enjoyed riding bicycles. Later, because of my declining vision, we sold our bikes and bought a tandem bicycle. Since a 'bicycle built for two' isn't a common sight, we got lots of smiles and waves – especially when we put our child in a seat on the back and all three of us would ride through our neighbourhood.

The person in the front seat on the bike is known as the captain or pilot. As the captain, my husband controlled the bike – steering, balancing and calling out instructions to me in the back, in the position called the stoker. My primary responsibility was to trust the pilot and provide as much power through the pedals as possible.

Using the tandem bike as an analogy for my spiritual journey, I understand that life works best when I give up control and trust God's guidance to steer and provide balance. I admit that sometimes I forget this truth and try to take control. Then I remember that just as the stoker listens for the instructions to lean into a turn or prepare for a bump in the road, I need to remember that God is in the pilot's seat. As Jesus assured his disciples, God assures me that I am riding in tandem and am never alone. God is always present on the journey.

Prayer: *Dear God, help us to let go and trust you as the one who is with us in every circumstance and moment of our journey. Amen*

Thought for the day: I may be the stoker, but God is the captain.

Karen E. Brown (Mississippi, US)

Away from the crowd

Read Matthew 6:5–15

Truly my soul finds rest in God; my salvation comes from him.
Psalm 62:1 (NIV)

My niece and her two young daughters were visiting us when the baby – about a year old – suddenly started crying. My niece took the baby to the bedroom to feed and comfort her. As I was thinking about this loving mother stepping away from the family gathering to feed her child, I remembered that sometimes God also calls us away from the crowd to a solitary place. Many times we do not understand what the call means or why God is calling.

Making room in our busy lives for solitude and time to be alone in prayer nurtures a vital relationship with God and equips us to meet the challenges and struggles of life. When we encounter sufferings – hardship, heartbreak, temptation, sickness or broken relationships – or even when we encounter new and exciting challenges, God calls us to be present as Christ teaches us to take his yoke upon ourselves and learn from him how to find rest for our souls. Spending time alone with God helps us to grow spiritually more and more into the likeness of Christ.

Prayer: *Dear Lord, help us to be alert to your 'still small voice' (1 Kings 19:12, KJV). Amen*

Thought for the day: Today I will treasure the time I spend with God.

Amod Pramanik (Odisha, India)

Sharing the good news

Read Romans 10:1–14

I pray that the sharing of your faith may become effective when you perceive all the good that we may do for Christ.
Philemon 1:6 (NRSV)

Because I have some hearing loss, I often miss or misunderstand what people say to me. Some people become irritated when I ask them to repeat things. I sometimes find myself feeling that what I have to say is not important enough to warrant frustrating others, so I am often reluctant to talk, especially to people I do not know well.

One day, God reminded me that even though I have trouble hearing I can still talk. I know Jesus as my Saviour and today's reading tells me to share my faith so that other people can know him too. I can share the good news about Jesus' birth in a lowly manger, how he healed many people, and how he died on the cross for all of us. I can share the promise of eternal life through Christ. This assurance is too important to keep to myself!

It's not always easy to talk to others about our faith, but we can trust God to show each of us our own way to share the good news of Christ with others.

Prayer: *Dear Lord, guide us to those who need to hear about you and grant us the courage to share the good news of your birth, death and resurrection with them. Amen*

Thought for the day: No matter what my limitations are, God can use me to share the gospel.

Donna J. Howard (Wisconsin, US)

PRAYER FOCUS: THOSE WITH HEARING LOSS

Obeying God

Read John 14:15–26

This is love: that we walk in obedience to [God's] commands. As you have heard from the beginning, his command is that you walk in love.
2 John 6 (NIV)

Now and then, my friend asks me to take care of his dog, a sweet, gentle and energetic pug. She's the kind of dog who doesn't need a lead. She rarely strays far from me, but if she does all I have to do is whistle and she runs back to me – tail wagging, happy to be with me. She instinctively obeys me because past experience has taught her that I won't hurt her.

When I am with her I often think of my walk with God. The Bible tells us that our lives will be full, rich and overflowing if we obey God's teachings and follow the example of the life of Jesus Christ. In God, 'we live and move and have our being' (see Acts 17:28). Every fibre of my body, heart and soul knows that I am secure in the loving embrace of my Creator God, who will never hurt me. In God, safety resides.

At times, obedience to God is not easy. But we can learn to be more obedient through prayer, a close study of scripture, and quiet time in God's presence. Then, when we fail, we can humble ourselves before him and ask for the gift of obedience. We will not always succeed, but ours is a forgiving God and nothing, absolutely nothing, will separate us from his love.

Prayer: *Creator God, help us to live daily as you would have us live – following the precepts you laid down long ago. Amen*

Thought for the day: Obedience to God brings love, peace and joy into my life.

Daniel C. Ladue (New York, US)

Doing it differently

Read John 21:1–6
Let us come boldly to the very throne of God.
Hebrews 4:16 (TLB)

After the crucifixion, when all seemed lost, the disciples returned to their old, familiar ways. They picked up their nets, set sail and went fishing. They worked hard all night, but they didn't catch anything. They'd had enough; they were bone tired. They had nothing to show – no fish, but more poignantly, nothing after all their sacrifices in following Jesus. It all seemed pointless.

Then Jesus came. He called to them, and told them to do something different. He told those expert fishermen to do what he said. And what a difference it made!

I identify with the disciples. I am weary. I work hard juggling my job and my carer role for my elderly mother. I have nothing to show for endless, mundane tasks. Then, through the words of a Communion service, I understood God's invitation to do something different.

The writer of Hebrews urges us to come boldly to the throne of God, so that we may receive his mercy and find grace to help us in our hour of need. Time and again since then, I have learnt to admit my inability to manage in my own strength. Time and again in my helplessness I draw near to God and receive his love, his strength and his grace.

We don't have to shoulder life's burdens alone. We can come boldly to God and receive from him.

Prayer: *Lord Jesus, I am spent and weary. In your all-sufficiency, please meet me in my need. Amen*

Thought for the day: Today I will receive God's grace to help me.

Hilary Allen (Somerset, England)

Small group questions

Wednesday 3 January

1 Describe a time when you felt God's presence guiding you through difficulty. Did you recognise his presence in your situation at the time or only when looking back on it? What did this experience teach you about God's faithfulness?

2 What scripture passages do you rely on during times of fear, worry or uncertainty? What practices help you to remember these passages? Which do you find most meaningful?

3 Recall a time when a community of Christians offered prayers for you. What was the situation? Did it make a difference that more than one person was praying for you? Do you think it affected the outcome of your situation?

4 What challenges are you facing today for which you would like the prayers of your church community?

5 Name one small action you can take to become more connected to Christians across the globe. What is your prayer for God's family of believers the world over?

Wednesday 10 January

1 When have you had a job or a role that felt mundane or even unimportant? When others asked you about this job, how did you describe it? Can you identify with the author's feelings?

2 Think about a time when you felt you were serving God joyfully. What were you doing? Who was with you? How could you serve God joyfully this week?

3 When you think about serving God joyfully or serving others with love, which Bible stories or characters come to mind?

4 What practices, prayers or Bible passages help you to remember God's presence in your daily life? What new practice will you incorporate into your day to help you be mindful of God?

5 At your church, who are the people whose work most often goes unnoticed? How can you express gratitude for their efforts?

Wednesday 17 January

1 How often do you read your Bible? Daily? Weekly? Do you find it hard to set time aside to read the Bible regularly? Why or why not?

2 Do you have a Bible you have treasured for many years? Do you, like the writer of today's meditation, write in the margins when you find a helpful verse or passage? If you do, how have these notes helped you?

3 How much do you rely on the Bible for guidance? Is the Bible the first place you go to if you need help with a particular problem? Why or why not?

4 What does it mean to say that the Bible is a light for our path? Does the Bible help us whatever our age or wherever we are in our Christian journey?

5 How much does your church community talk about the importance of the Bible in everyday life? Can you think of ways that this can be expanded to help people in their use of the Bible each day?

Wednesday 24 January

1 Do you believe that experiencing pain and suffering – both emotional and physical – serves a purpose? Do you think God ever wants us to suffer? Why or why not?

2 Today's 'Thought for the day' says, 'Healing may come slowly, but God is with me through it all.' Talk about a time in your life when God was with you 'through it all'.

3 What role does God have in healing us? What role do we have in our own healing? Why do you think healing comes quickly for some people and not at all for others?

4 The quoted scripture verse for today's meditation invites us to pour our hearts out to God. When was the last time you poured your heart out to God? What did you say to him?

5 Who in your church community needs prayers of healing today? How often will you pray for them in the coming week? For what will you pray?

Wednesday 31 January

1 What do you think about the exchange on the bus between the man and the writer's friend Sheila? Have you ever had a similar conversation with someone? Describe the experience. What did you learn from it?

2 When have you felt that you were in exactly the place God wanted you to be? Where were you? What made you feel that God wanted you there?

3 In what ways do you prepare yourself to share the gospel with others? Is there such a thing as a right time and a wrong time to share the gospel with another person? Why or why not?

4 Have you ever tried to share your faith with someone only to offend the person? How did the person respond to you? Why was he or she offended? Should we be concerned whether we offend others when trying to share our faith with them?

5 Are there ways we can share the love, sacrifice and redemption that Jesus offers without talking about them directly? If so, what are they? In your opinion, what is the best way to share your faith with others?

Wednesday 7 February

1 Would you describe yourself as a patient or impatient person? Do you think it is OK to be impatient in some situations? If so, when and why?

2 How well do you identify with the frustration of the writer of today's meditation? Have you shown frustration in similar circumstances? How do you think God wants us to act when we become frustrated?

3 Name some characters from scripture who were impatient. Retell their stories in your own words. With which of these characters' attributes do you relate most closely? What do their stories teach us about impatience?

4 Today's writer says, 'Every moment – even a frustrating moment waiting at a pizza counter – is sacred.' What do you think she means by this statement? Do you agree with her? Why or why not?

5 When in a moment of stress or frustration have you shown compassion and grace to someone? Was this easy or difficult for you? Why was it easy (or difficult)? What does scripture say about extending compassion and grace to others?

Wednesday 14 February

1 Describe a time when you have sensed God directing your life. What was this experience like? What did you learn from it? To what was God directing you?

2 Do you think that God has a unique purpose for each of our lives? How can we discover what God's purpose for our life is?

3 Have you ever felt as if you have lost your sense of purpose in life? How did you regain your sense of purpose? What advice would you give to others who feel the same?

4 When have you felt unworthy or insecure about something? Were you able to overcome these feelings? If so, how did you overcome them? If not, what prevents you from overcoming them?

5 Name some New Testament characters who lacked education, experience, and/or social status but played an important part in spreading the gospel. What do these characters teach us about whom God chooses to do his work in the world?

Wednesday 21 February

1 With whom can you share your deepest thoughts without fear of judgement or criticism? How did you come to know this person? How often do you see him or her? What does this relationship mean to you?

2 When have you been a friend to someone with whom they can share their deepest thoughts? Is it easy or difficult for you to be this kind of friend to someone? What has this friendship taught you about yourself?

3 The writer of today's meditation says, '[God] never sends me away empty but instead fills my cup and feeds me the bread of life that my soul hungers for.' What do you think she means by this statement? Speak about a time in your life when this has been true for you.

4 Are there any topics or situations in your life that are difficult to talk to God about? What are they? Why is it hard for you to talk to him about them?

5 How much time do you spend with God each day? What do you do when spending time with him? Read scripture? Pray? Meditate? What keeps you from spending more time with God each day?

Wednesday 28 February

1 How closely can you relate to the doubt and scepticism of today's writer? Explain your answer.

2 Is it OK for Christians to have doubts? Who in scripture had doubts? How did God respond to them? What can we learn from their stories?

3 Have you ever been uncomfortable when another Christian has asked you questions or expressed doubts about his or her faith? What was the situation? Why did this person's questions or doubts make you uncomfortable? How did you respond?

4 Do you have any doubts of your own that you are willing to share with others? If so, what are they?

5 If you could ask God one question about anything – nothing is off limits – what would it be?

Wednesday 7 March

1 Is being quiet something that comes naturally to you? Why or why not?

2 Would you describe yourself as an introvert or an extrovert? How does this shape your relationship with God? What does spending time with him look like for you?

3 The writer of today's meditation says, 'When I pray, I have found it easier to speak aloud to God as though speaking to a human friend. My quiet time can also include singing.' Do you agree that 'quiet time' can include speaking aloud and singing? Explain.

4 Have you experienced a time in your life during which it was difficult to pray? What was the situation? Why was it difficult to pray? How did you get through it?

5 Were you to commit to spending quiet time with God each day this week, what would your quiet time include?

Wednesday 14 March

1 Today's quoted verse (1 Peter 5:7) says, 'Cast all your anxiety on [God], because he cares for you.' What does it mean for us to cast all our anxiety on God? Do you think it is easier for some people to give their worries to him than it is for others? Does it get any easier with practice? Is it possible to live completely free from worry? Why or why not?

2 Can you relate to the statement, 'The weight of our struggles piles on so gradually that we often don't realise how it is affecting us'? Talk about a time in your life when this has been true for you. What did you learn from this experience?

3 How do you usually observe Lent? Do you give something up or take something on? Can you recall a Lent that was particularly meaningful for you? Why was it meaningful?

4 How are you observing this Lenten season? What do you hope to accomplish or learn?

5 Name some of the burdens that you are carrying with you today for which you would like the prayers of your church community.

Wednesday 21 March

1 Have you ever doubted God's presence during a difficult situation? Why was it hard to trust that he was there? What will you do differently the next time you are in a similar situation?

2 The 'Thought for the day' says, 'Though I cannot see God with my eyes, I know that he is always near.' Describe a time when you were confident God was near even though you could not see him with your eyes.

3 Is it ever OK to doubt God's presence in our lives? Why or why not? Give examples from scripture to support your answer.

4 When have you felt most distant from God? In what ways did this time in your life challenge you? What opportunities for growth did it provide?

5 When do you feel closest to God? During a church service? While participating in community outreach? In a small-group Bible study? At some other event or location?

Wednesday 28 March

1 When has someone ministered to you in a powerful way? What was going on in your life at the time? How did this person minister to you?

2 Who do you turn to or depend on when you have a bad day or go through a life-challenge? What does this person do that helps you?

3 Have you ever prayed for God to intervene in a difficult situation? What was the outcome of the situation? Did God intervene? What did you learn from the experience? How did this experience affect your relationship with him?

4 Do you agree with the writer of today's meditation when she says

that 'God is concerned with every small detail of our lives'? Why or why not? Give an example from your life to support your answer.

5   Who in your church community needs ministering to today? What will you do to help this person? How will you show this person that he or she is loved?

Wednesday 4 April

1   Have you ever had a loved one depend on you for care? What helped you keep a positive attitude while caring for this person? What advice would you give to someone caring for a loved one today?

2   When has God called you to do something that you did not want to do? What was he calling you to do? Did you do it? Why do you think God sometimes calls us to do things that we don't want to do?

3   Name some characters from scripture who were called to do things they did not want to do. How did they respond to God's call? What do their stories teach us?

4   What are some specific things you do to keep your faith alive and your relationship with God strong during hard times?

5   Read Galatians 6:9 – today's quoted verse – three times aloud. What word or phrase from this verse jumps out at you? Why does it jump out at you? What in this verse encourages you?

Wednesday 11 April

1   The writer of today's meditation tells how he came to faith in Christ. Take a few minutes to tell the story of how you came to faith in Christ. How are your story and the writer's alike? How are they different?

2   Who has been the most influential person to you on your Christian journey? How has this person influenced you, and what do you admire most about him or her?

3   Do you agree that there is a difference between being happy and being joyful? Explain your answer.

4   What does it look like in a person's life to find 'joy in the Lord'? What can someone who is not a Christian and has never been to church before do to find 'joy in the Lord'? What words of hope and strength would you offer this person?

5   Can you remember when you were a new Christian? What is most memorable from that time in your life? Who did you rely on for strength and support? How can you support new Christians in your church community today?

Wednesday 18 April

1   What difference does it make in our Christian walk that God calls us by name? How does it affect the way we treat other people? How does it affect our relationship with God?

2   How personal is your relationship with God? Name some ways in which your relationship with him could be more personal. Can our relationship with God ever be too personal?

3   Name some scripture passages that speak about God's love for each of us. Which of these do you find most meaningful? Why?

4   Who in your life needs to know that God calls him or her by name? What can you do to fill this need?

5   Which group of people in the world do you have difficulty seeing as individuals with their own fears, losses, hopes and loves? Why is it a challenge to see the people in this group as individuals? What can you do to help yourself see every person as someone who is loved by God?

Wednesday 25 April

1   Were you brought up in a Christian home? Do you think being brought up in a Christian home makes someone a better Christian than those who come to faith in Christ later in life? Why or why not?

2   Have you ever known anyone like Reverend Zuhl or Eileen in today's meditation? What qualities of this person would you like to emulate

in your own life? For whom could you be a Reverend Zuhl or Eileen today?

3   Describe what you think it means for a person's life to be 'grounded in the Lord'. How do we know when our life is 'grounded in the Lord'?

4   When has an experience changed the course of your faith journey? How has this experience shaped your walk with Christ?

5   What opportunities for ministry can you participate in today? In what specific ways can you share the gift of God's love with others? Where and with whom will you share this gift?

Journal page

Journal page

Journal page

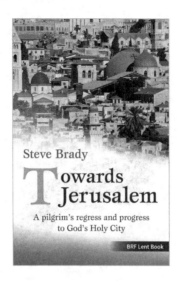

God has an agenda for cities. Steve Brady is convinced of it. The Bible is full of significant cities and the biblical story is full of imagery of cities – culminating in God's Holy City, birthed in and through his people. *Towards Jerusalem* is a unique Lent book, a call to live for a vision bigger than ourselves, marching to a different drumbeat towards 'Zion', God's new Jerusalem, and all that this means in transformative terms for today's Christian believer.

Towards Jerusalem
A pilgrim's regress and progress to God's Holy City
Steve Brady
978 0 85746 560 3 £7.99
brfonline.org.uk

In *Seasoned by Seasons*, Michael Mitton offers Bible reflections for the variety of life's seasons: spring, the season of emerging new life; summer, the season of fruitfulness; autumn, the season of letting go; winter, the season of discovering light in the dark. What can we learn, and how can we be encouraged in each season of our lives? This book will empower you to discover for yourself the truths and messages of scripture, and might well transform the way you view life's changes.

Seasoned by Seasons
Flourishing in life's experiences
Michael Mitton
978 0 85746 540 5 £7.99
brfonline.org.uk

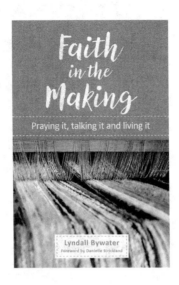

If faith is 'being sure of what we hope for and certain of what we do not see', what does that look like in practice today? In a world that is largely unsure and uncertain, how do we gain our confidence? *Faith in the Making* recognises the problem and seeks the answer in the list of faithful heroes found in Hebrews 11. This accessible, devotional resource will inspire individuals and groups to live more confidently for God in today's world. Heroic faith is far more attainable than we often think!

Faith in the Making
Praying it, talking it and living it
Lyndall Bywater, with a foreword by Danielle Strickland
978 0 85746 555 9 £7.99
brfonline.org.uk

Where do we turn when our world is falling apart? It takes courage to
hope: to stand in our confusion and grief and still to believe that 'God
is not helpless among the ruins'. Guided by Habakkuk and his prophetic
landmarks, this book is a reflective journey through the tangled landscape
of bewildered faith, through places of wrestling and waiting, and on into
the growth space of deepened trust and transformation. Read it and
learn the value and practice of honest prayer, of surrender, of silence and
listening, and of irresistible hoping.

God among the Ruins
Trust and transformation in difficult times
Mags Duggan, with a foreword by Tony Horsfall
978 0 85746 575 7 £7.99
brfonline.org.uk

How to encourage Bible reading in your church

BRF has been helping individuals connect with the Bible for over 90 years. We want to support churches as they seek to encourage church members into regular Bible reading.

Order a Bible reading resources pack

This pack is designed to give your church the tools to publicise our Bible reading notes. It includes:

- Sample Bible reading notes for your congregation to try.
- Publicity resources, including a poster.
- A church magazine feature about Bible reading notes.

The pack is free, but we welcome a £5 donation to cover the cost of postage. If you require a pack to be sent outside the UK or require a specific number of sample Bible reading notes, please contact us for postage costs. More information about what the current pack contains is available on our website.

How to order and find out more

- Visit **biblereadingnotes.org.uk/for-churches**.
- Telephone BRF on +44 (0)1865 319700 Mon–Fri 9.15–17.30.
- Write to us at BRF, 15 The Chambers, Vineyard, Abingdon OX14 3FE.

Keep informed about our latest initiatives

We are continuing to develop resources to help churches encourage people into regular Bible reading, wherever they are on their journey. Join our email list at **biblereadingnotes.org.uk/helpingchurches** to stay informed about the latest initiatives that your church could benefit from.

Introduce a friend to our notes

We can send information about our notes and current prices for you to pass on. Please contact us.

Subscriptions

The Upper Room is published in January, May and September.

Individual subscriptions
The subscription rate for orders for 4 or fewer copies includes postage and packing:
The Upper Room annual individual subscription   £16.95

Group subscriptions
Orders for 5 copies or more, sent to ONE address, are post free:
The Upper Room annual group subscription   £13.50

Please do not send payment with order for a group subscription. We will send an invoice with your first order.

Please note that the annual billing period for group subscriptions runs from 1 May to 30 April.

Copies of the notes may also be obtained from Christian bookshops.

Single copies of *The Upper Room* cost £4.50.

Prices valid until 30 April 2019.

Giant print version
The Upper Room is available in giant print for the visually impaired, from:

Torch Trust for the Blind
Torch House
Torch Way
Northampton Road
Market Harborough   Tel: +44 (0)1858 438260
LE16 9HL   torchtrust.org

THE UPPER ROOM: INDIVIDUAL/GIFT SUBSCRIPTION FORM

All our Bible reading notes can be ordered online by visiting biblereadingnotes.org.uk/subscriptions

❑ I would like to take out a subscription myself (complete your name and address details once)
❑ I would like to give a gift subscription (please provide both names and addresses)

Title .... First name/initials .... Surname ....

Address ....

.... Postcode ....

Telephone .... Email ....

Gift subscription name ....

Gift subscription address ....

.... Postcode ....

Gift message (20 words max. or include your own gift card):

....

....

Please send *The Upper Room* beginning with the May 2018 / September 2018 / January 2019 issue (delete as appropriate):

Annual individual subscription ❑ £16.95   Total enclosed £ ....

Please keep me informed about BRF's books and resources ❑ by email ❑ by post
Please keep me informed about the wider work of BRF ❑ by email ❑ by post

Method of payment

❑ Cheque (made payable to BRF)   ❑ MasterCard / Visa

Card no. ⬚⬚⬚⬚ ⬚⬚⬚⬚ ⬚⬚⬚⬚ ⬚⬚⬚⬚

Valid from ⬚⬚ ⬚⬚   Expires ⬚⬚ ⬚⬚

Security code* ⬚⬚⬚   *Last 3 digits on the reverse of the card
ESSENTIAL IN ORDER TO PROCESS THE PAYMENT

THE UPPER ROOM GROUP SUBSCRIPTION FORM

**All our Bible reading notes can be ordered online by visiting
biblereadingnotes.org.uk/subscriptions**

☐ Please send me .... copies of *The Upper Room* May 2018 / September 2018 /
January 2019 issue (*delete as appropriate*)

Title .... First name/initials .... Surname ....
Address ....
.... Postcode ....
Telephone .... Email ....

Please do not send payment with this order. We will send an invoice with your first order.

Christian bookshops: All good Christian bookshops stock BRF publications. For your
nearest stockist, please contact BRF.

Telephone: The BRF office is open Mon–Fri 9.15–17.30. To place your order, telephone
+44 (0)1865 319700.

Online: brf.org.uk

☐ Please send me a Bible reading resources pack to encourage Bible reading in
my church

Please return this form with the appropriate payment to:
BRF, 15 The Chambers, Vineyard, Abingdon OX14 3FE

To read our terms and find out about cancelling your order, please visit **brfonline.org.uk/terms**.

The Bible Reading Fellowship is a Registered Charity (233280)

UR0118

To order

Online: **brfonline.org.uk**
Telephone: +44 (0)1865 319700
Mon–Fri 9.15–17.30

Delivery times within the UK are normally
15 working days. Prices are correct at the time of
going to press but may change without prior notice.

Title	Price	Qty	Total
Towards Jerusalem	7.99		
Seasoned by Seasons	7.99		
Faith in the Making	7.99		
God among the Ruins	7.99		

POSTAGE AND PACKING CHARGES			
Order value	UK	Europe	Rest of world
Under £7.00	£2.00	£5.00	£7.00
£7.00–£29.99	£3.00	£9.00	£15.00
£30.00 and over	FREE	£9.00 + 15% of order value	£15.00 + 20% of order value

Total value of books	
Postage and packing	
Donation	
Total for this order	

Please complete in BLOCK CAPITALS

Title .... First name/initials .... Surname ....

Address ....

.... Postcode ....

Acc. No. .... Telephone ....

Email ....

Please keep me informed about BRF's books and resources ☐ by email ☐ by post
Please keep me informed about the wider work of BRF ☐ by email ☐ by post

Method of payment

☐ Cheque (made payable to BRF) ☐ MasterCard / Visa

Card no. ☐☐☐☐ ☐☐☐☐ ☐☐☐☐ ☐☐☐☐

Valid from [M][M] [Y][Y] Expires [M][M] [Y][Y] Security code* ☐☐☐
Last 3 digits on the reverse of the card

Signature* .... Date .... /.......... /..........
*ESSENTIAL IN ORDER TO PROCESS YOUR ORDER

The Bible Reading Fellowship Gift Aid Declaration

giftaid it

Please treat as Gift Aid donations all qualifying gifts of money made
☐ today, ☐ in the past four years, ☐ and in the future **or** ☐ My donation does not qualify for Gift Aid.
I am a UK taxpayer and understand that if I pay less Income Tax and/or Capital Gains Tax in the current tax
year than the amount of Gift Aid claimed on all my donations, it is my responsibility to pay any difference.
Please notify BRF if you want to cancel this declaration, change your name or home address, or no longer
pay sufficient tax on your income and/or capital gains.

Please return this form to: BRF, 15 The Chambers, Vineyard, Abingdon OX14 3FE | enquiries@brf.org.uk
To read our terms and find out about cancelling your order, please visit **brfonline.org.uk/terms**.

Transforming
lives and communities

Christian growth and understanding of the Bible

Resourcing individuals, groups and leaders in churches for their own spiritual journey and for their ministry

Church outreach in the local community

Offering three programmes that churches are embracing
to great effect as they seek to engage
with their local communities
and transform lives

Teaching Christianity in primary schools

Working with children and teachers to explore Christianity creatively and confidently

Children's and family ministry

Working with churches and families to explore Christianity creatively and bring the Bible alive

Visit **brf.org.uk** for more information on BRF's work
Review this book on Twitter using **#BRFconnect**

brf.org.uk